Praise for ANXIETY:

"Dr. Katherine Kelly's book is a clear, original and important analysis of the ways in which conventional approaches to the classification and treatment of anxiety disorders falls woefully short of treating the whole person by its exclusion of the essential component of illness related to the soul. She proposes an expanded holistic model which delineates an understanding and treatment of illness that includes the body, mind, and soul. This book provides much needed medicine for our soul sick world."

–Judy Tsafrir, M.D., Psychiatrist and author of *Sacred Psychiatry: Bridging the Personal and Transpersonal to Transform Health and Consciousness*

"Are you seeking to heal anxiety at the deepest level to create truly transformational results? Dr. Katherine T. Kelly's brilliant Whole Soul Model is a rarity—a truly holistic approach to understanding the human condition and avenues for healing and growth that includes what's so often missing: the influence of the soul. Clinicians and readers who are ready to venture beyond the conventional understanding of anxiety will love this book."

–Mark Bottinick, LCSW-C, Licensed Clinical Social Worker

"Finally! Someone did it! Dr. Kelly so eloquently and intelligently synced the two worlds of professional psychotherapy with spiritual soul healing as it relates to our ever-expanding mental health crisis of anxiety. I cannot wait for the rest of the series! As a therapist and spiritual soul healing practitioner, I have deeply studied spiritual healing and shamanic healing practices as a means to heal myself and better understand healing as a whole. Once I did, my work with clients became richer, deeper, and more profound for them and for me as the provider. I believe this is a crucial direction our field needs to take."

–Angela Eischens, MA, LMFT, Licensed Marriage and Family Therapist, Reiki Master Practitioner

"Dr. Kelly and her book are mending what through many years has wrongly been separated and isolated from the healing of the human being. Within my practice of energy work in the human biofield, the most consistent desire of my clients is to be whole in their purpose. I see Dr. Kelly's book as a significant guiding tool in healing, giving the long-needed support of the Soul to the body and the mind."

–Loretta Childress, BA, M.A.T., Certified Biofield Tuning Practitioner (Advanced), Reiki Master, Cymatherapy Practitioner

"Even within an era of evidence-based and manualized treatment protocols, anxiety remains one of the most challenging conditions to effectively treat. Dr. Kelly offers a more complete approach to conceptualizing and treating anxiety by expanding her Soul Health Model into the Whole Soul Model. By elevating the most important part of who we are in our understanding of the human condition, Dr. Kelly provides a roadmap for whole person healing at a time when it is needed the most."

–Joseph R. Biggs, Ph.D., HSPP, Licensed Psychologist

"Dr. Katherine Kelly creates a soul-based paradigm for healing, bringing new meaning to the phrase 'just what the doctor ordered.' It is so refreshing and needed to see this emerging and taking its place in mental health. This book provides facts on the history of disease and treatments and Dr. Kelly's soul-fortifying approach to health and wellness. Her exploration of alternative methods has truly elevated her practice as well as the reader seeking a holistic approach to healing."

–Herb Hernandez, Astrologer, Holistic Wellness Coach, Certified in Plant Based Nutrition

"In *Anxiety*, the first book in her *Soul of Psychology Series*, Dr. Katherine Kelly insightfully points out that western medicine's lack of 'soul tending' is the missing link when addressing tough-to-treat mental (and physical) health issues. Love and conflict, life and death, fear and hope, spirit, and body are all factors of illness, yet our healthcare system is not structured around these aspects. Dr. Kelly's soul-informed approach to treating anxiety-related disorders convincingly shows practitioners and patients the importance of valuing the state of the soul as part of the healing process."

–Bridget Budd, Trauma-informed Life Coach,
Holistic Health Coach, Yoga Practitioner

"Dr. Katherine Kelly's Whole Soul Health Model is exactly what I had been looking for. She clearly illustrates that for true healing to occur, it needs to happen on the soul level. I had been doing this level of healing with my own clients but struggled to explain it in a way that made sense. Dr. Kelly has a beautiful and eloquent way of describing the layers of healing with anxiety in a way that is easily understood. This book guides healers from all walks of life in helping others heal from a soul level, reconnecting them with their joy, and ultimately changing the human condition in profound ways."

–Bryn Lowrie Yahn, Ph.D., Licensed Psychologist

"As a therapist, I found this book insightful and a refreshing message about adapting a holistic lens to treatment. It is inspirational to the field of psychology, which often teaches about the importance of looking at the 'whole picture' but fails to emphasize the need to be open-minded to other approaches to understand a person on a deeper level. While evidence-based treatment has proven effective, too often we get caught up in needing tangible evidence to confirm what the simple act of listening and offering space can quickly tell us. It is a must-have read for any budding or seasoned therapist."

–Aida Morales, LPC, Licensed Professional Counselor

"This book is a pragmatic bridge between the current treatments and methodologies of addressing anxiety disorders, and a deeper understanding of the core role the soul plays in the full healing process of the human body. Like the soul that exists in the unseen realm and silently weaves its presence through one's daily life, the reader will find subtle and powerful truths weaving through the space between the words of Dr. Kelly's insightful book."

–Donna Chimera, Personal and Business Coach,
Former Licensed Nursing Home Administrator

"Anxiety has become such a common term and condition. As a bodywork therapist in the preventative healthcare world and a mom of three teenage daughters, anxiety symptoms are often presented to me as something more people have trouble managing or controlling. Dr. Kelly's book has already helped me gain a deeper understanding of anxiety and insight into getting to the soul root of the problem!"

–Michele Bishop, Licensed Massage and Bodywork Therapist

"This is a beautifully written book designed to help readers understand the context of anxiety through the lens of the soul. It is designed to assist mental health clinicians and individuals recognize how patterns of anxiety may be related to the soul, as well as ways to address those soul patterns psychologically. This is a must read for anyone wishing to understand the deepest roots of anxiety and how to heal them more fully."

–Amber W. Pearson, MA, LPC, LCMHC, LMHC,
Licensed Mental Health Counselor

ANXIETY
Treating Body, Mind and Soul

The Soul of Psychology Series
Book One

ANXIETY
Treating Body, Mind and Soul

Dr. Katherine T. Kelly
Ph.D., M.S.P.H.

SOUL HEALTH
PRESS

Winston-Salem, North Carolina

Copyright © 2024 by Katherine T. Kelly

All rights reserved. No part of this book may be used or reproduced by any means, graphic, electronic, or mechanical, including photocopying, recording, taping or by any information storage retrieval system without the written permission of the publisher except in the case of brief quotations embodied in critical articles and reviews.

Soul Health Press books may be ordered through booksellers or by contacting Soul Health Press, www.soulhealthpress.com

To contact the author about speaking, workshops, or bulk orders of this book, visit https://drkatherinetkelly.com

Because of the dynamic nature of the Internet, any web addresses or links contained in this book may have changed since publication and may no longer be valid.

This book contains the opinions and ideas of its author. Although the author and publisher have made every effort to ensure that the information in this book was correct at press time, no liability is assumed for losses or damages due to the information provided.

The author of this book does not dispense medical advice or prescribe the use of any technique as a form of treatment for physical, emotional, or medical problems without the advice of a physician (or other qualified healthcare, mental health, or holistic health professional), either directly or indirectly. The author's intent is to offer information of a general nature to help you in the quest for emotional and spiritual well-being.

ISBN (paperback): 978-1-964139-00-5
ISBN (hardcover): 978-1-964139-01-2
ISBN (ebook): 978-1-964139-02-9

Editor: Carol Hildebrandt

Book cover and interior design: Christy Day, Constellation Book Services

Library of Congress Control Number: 202490640

Printed in the United States of America

To the soul side of life.

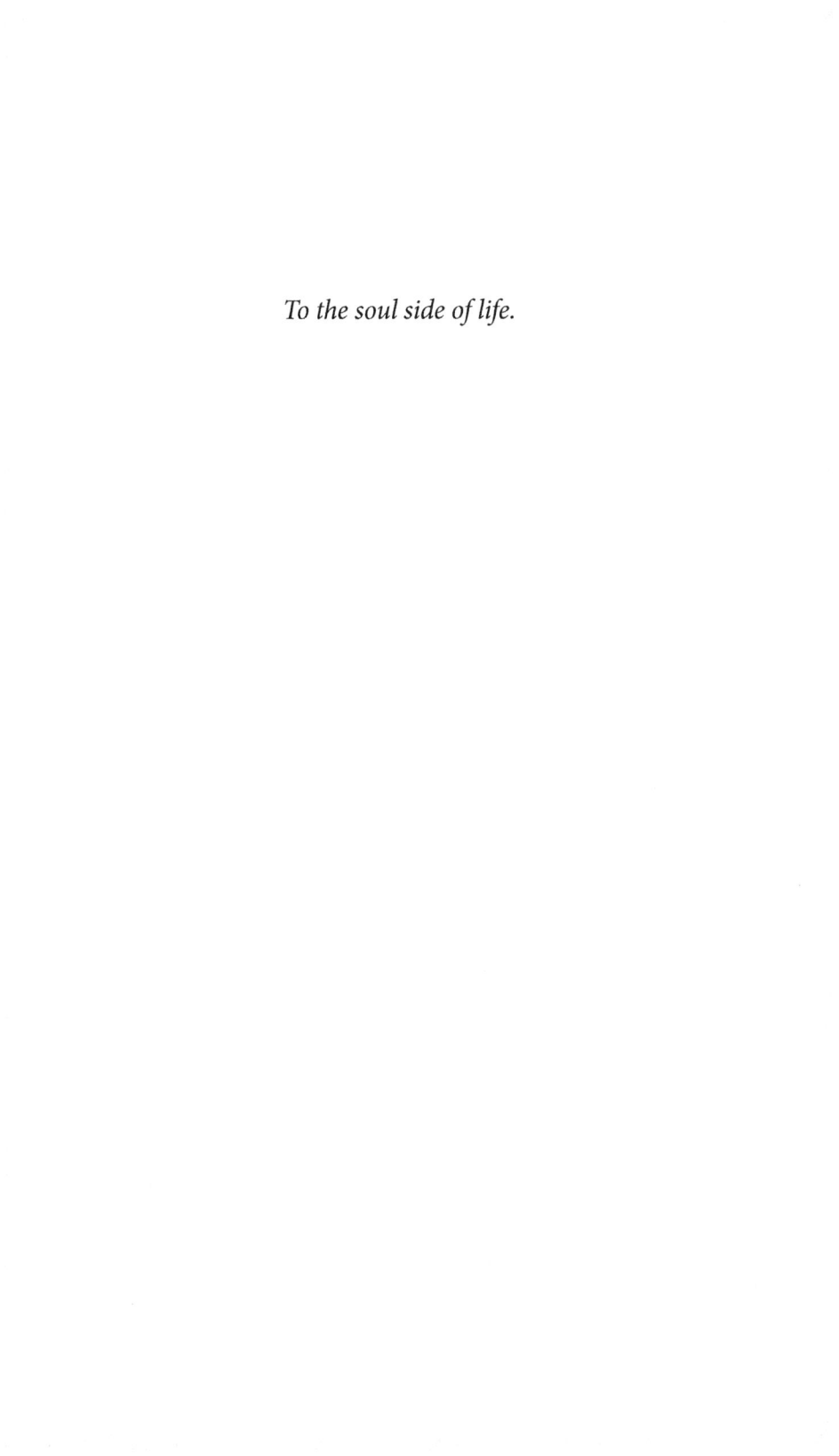

CONTENTS

Acknowledgments   *xv*
A Note from the Author   1

PART ONE: The History of Healing Anxiety   **11**
   Chapter One: Soul Origins of Anxiety   13
   Chapter Two: The Psyche and the Soul   25
   Chapter Three: The Evolution of Modern Anxiety   37
   Chapter Four: Treating the Body and Modern Anxiety   59
   Chapter Five: Treating the Mind and Modern Anxiety   83
   Chapter Six: The Three Levels of Healing   99

PART TWO: The Soul Side of Anxiety   **113**
   Chapter Seven: The Evolution of Soul Healing   115
   Chapter Eight: Soul Health and the Manifestation of Anxiety   125
   Chapter Nine: Understanding Anxiety Through the Soul Side of Health   147
   Chapter Ten: Healing the Roots of Anxiety   165

PART THREE: Anxiety: The New Treatment Paradigm   **183**
   Chapter Eleven: Soul-Informed Care: A Whole Soul Approach to Understanding Anxiety   185
   Chapter Twelve: Soul-Based Modalities to Assist in the Treatment of Anxiety   205
   Chapter Thirteen: Seeking Whole Soul Treatment of Anxiety   223
   Chapter Fourteen: Integrative Care: Body, Mind and Soul Treatment of Anxiety   239

Post Script   *253*
References   *257*

True healing is when the soul is at peace.
RUMI

ACKNOWLEDGMENTS

The soul is life. It is the part of us that lives on regardless of the state of our body or mind. It is also the part that connects us to others—the souls who season our own.

Every day, I pause to acknowledge those who have touched the essence of who I am, whether through support, love, lessons or laughter—sometimes all of these mixed into one. With each experience and acknowledgement, I grow. I am forever grateful for each soul—human and other—with whom I've crossed paths as each teaches me more about both myself and the "soul side" of our evolutionary journey. I would not be who I am without these cherished moments and I would not have the privilege of living either my life passion or soul's purpose without these enriching encounters.

I'm deeply grateful to have worked with so many to assist them on their own soul-healing journey. Through serving you, I am served. There is nothing better for me than to watch souls evolve and each day I am amazed that I am so immensely blessed. Thank you for the honor and privilege of allowing me to guide and support you on your evolutionary path.

I've been asked how I have accumulated my knowledge and I generally don't know how to answer. My soul has been seasoned by so many authors, teachers, philosophers, educators, supervisors, fellow students, practitioners, colleagues, spiritual teachers and leaders, poets, songwriters, artists, retreat leaders, park rangers, arborists, baristas, grocery store clerks, neighbors, massage therapists, homeless citizens, animals, chance encounters (although these are never "by chance"), observations of people walking down the street or sitting on a bench, life experiences, soulful occurrences, spiritual expeditions—both planned an unplanned, and of course, friends, family, soul group members, and beloved pets that I don't know specifically who to thank. Instead, I will say I'm deeply grateful for everyone who so deliciously seasons my soul. You generally know who you are anyway.

Special thanks go to my literary "soul health team". First, much gratitude goes to Martha Bullen, my literary consultant (aka "The Fire Engine") who both gets my attention and gets things done. You've seen me through four book launches so far with many more to come. You've taught me much. I'm fortunate to not only call you a colleague, but also a friend.

Deep gratitude also goes to Christy Day, who so beautifully completed the cover and internal design for this book and played a key role in developing the "body, mind and soul" tree image for the *Soul of Psychology* book series. You helped to birth a new grove of tree images into my soul health forest. Thank you!

Ongoing thanks goes to Carol Hildebrandt, medical editor, word master and conceptual cheerleader who continues to help me hone my own writing skills. Our brief encounter years ago led to an ongoing partnership now and I couldn't be happier with your work. Your expertise, along with your ongoing feedback and support are priceless. I'm deeply grateful.

Continued gratitude goes to Chara Murray, graphic genius extraordinaire. After nearly two decades of creating my soul health forest (and a very thick binder of images!), I'm fortunate to call you a fun and cherished friend. I appreciate your humor, creative mastery, patience, flexibility and never-ending "noodling" of concepts, ideas and images. All I can say is, don't go anywhere. We have more work to do!

I also want to thank my growing network of soul-based practitioners and colleagues who are also on a mission to bring the soul back to mainstream thinking and experience. Soul-Informed Care is necessary to fully heal the wounds of the human condition. There is truly power in numbers and not only have I loved getting to know you, I'm also fortunate to learn from you as well. In knowing you, I stay humble in realizing that there is so much more to know. Thank you.

Light and love goes to every soul who reads this book or any other I offer. Whether you are someone who chooses to explore and integrate the soul into your healing process or are a practitioner, coach, educator or administrator, wishing to understand more about the soul to serve others, I hope you find what you need to enhance your own soul health journey.

It is time to bring the soul back into the light. Together, we will honor the body, mind **and** soul in the process of healing.

A NOTE FROM THE AUTHOR

Most people don't know that fields of both medicine and psychology began with the soul. In the early 400s BC Hippocrates, the father of medicine, stated that every physical condition manifested through the influence of this internal force. In the early 1900s Carl Jung, one of the founding fathers of psychology, emphasized that the psyche was formed through what he called the collective unconscious—an inherent understanding of both symbols and meaning of personal or cultural effects that couldn't have been known through experience in the current life alone. The soul became a central focus of his work. Both Hippocrates and Jung knew that something other than the body and mind animated our motivations within the human condition.

Today, both fields generally operate under the modern assumption that the biopsychosocial approach is enough. This method takes into consideration that biology, psychology and the impact of our social interactions explain the entirety of both our experience as humans and how most conditions are treated. However, given the current state of healthcare as well as the explosion of mental health conditions in society, something is seriously missing. The most important part of who we are has been omitted from both the conceptualization and treatment of all medical and mental health concerns.

Almost two decades ago, I created *The Soul Health Model*™, a comprehensive wellness paradigm that serves as a blueprint or roadmap for helping an individual heal and balance their life. Prior examples only incorporated a handful of aspects that impact a person's health. However, after many years of work in medical psychology, mental health and wellness, I realized many "branches" or aspects of overall wellbeing were missing. I also recognized that the driving force of all of these components had never been explained in contemporary health-related models. To me, something was fundamentally wrong with the way in which both medical and mental healthcare was provided.

After creating the model, I taught various healthcare professionals around the country how to incorporate a more complete approach to caring for those they served. The feedback and appreciation I received was astounding. Most said they'd never recognized that so many components had been missing from their studies and also stated that the core aspect of each individual—the *soul*—had never been considered as part of their treatment. One professional asked if I'd ever thought about creating a certification program for healthcare professionals to learn to work *The Soul Health Model*™ into their provision of care. At the time, it hadn't crossed my mind, but I am now in the process of developing specialized training for practitioners, coaches, educators and administrators as a result of that conversation. The soul can no longer be left out of healthcare if we are going to fill the largest gap in how services are currently provided.

When I created the model, I had no idea how far it would go. In the midst of the deadliest part of the COVID-19 pandemic, I interviewed nearly one hundred and fifty healthcare workers to write a book to help them rebuild their lives once they had the time and energy to recover. I provided the model to each of them, along with a set of sample questions to get their minds stirring. Many of them shared that both the model and list of questions gave them hope that a time would come when they could restore, possibly in a whole new way. One physician wrote a few months after the book was published to say the model and our conversations had saved his life. Even in the depth of his despair he hadn't realized how much of his life force was gone. Without a new understanding of how to resuscitate his soul, he wouldn't have had the tools to recover, let alone to live. He admitted he might not be here had our paths not crossed.

Over the last year, hundreds of medical and mental health providers have somehow found me and asked to either meet to discuss what I do or to be added to my email list so they could be the first to know about the certifications I'm creating. In just the last two weeks over one hundred more have asked to join an online networking group I started called *The Soul of Healing Collaborative Group* (on Alignable.com). And just last week, a new psychotherapy client—a physician who experienced some traumatic events during her training said my explanation of the soul in her healing process was the first thing that made sense, even after undergoing years of previous psychological treatment. The world is ready for a deeper form of healing.

Over the years, I've studied many forms of holistic health and healing strategies. While many have included training about natural treatment of mental health concerns, multiple others have focused on various soul-healing strategies. I'm amazed at how much further clients can go and how much deeper their healing is when I incorporate a "whole soul experience" approach to care. I've been doing this for so long that I barely remembered that others don't take this approach.

The Soul of Psychology book series evolved from the awareness that others need a better understanding of not only the body and mind components of healing, but most importantly the *soul* aspects as well. These factors inevitably influence both the manifestation and healing of mental health concerns, as well as many physical conditions that aren't otherwise easily explained. Once the "soul side" of our experience is understood, the more complete and sustainable healing becomes.

Anxiety: Treating Body, Mind and Soul is the first of several books in the series to explain how our inner self—the driving force within— needs attention in the process of both treatment and healing. Like all other mental health concerns, the treatment of anxiety has lacked a key element ever since the fields of modern medicine and psychology were established as the primary options for addressing emotional concerns. While evidence-based action related to the body and mind aspects of anxiety disorders is necessary to identify and manage symptoms, it is often insufficient in returning a patient to a state of whole health. Frequently, it is the less known *soul-based* origin and soul-healing methods for treating an anxiety disorder that must be addressed to help a person feel complete.

This book offers a comprehensive view of the origins of many anxiety-related concerns and emphasizes deeper aspects that may have created the initial emotional disturbance or may block full healing when traditional methods aren't enough. Source factors such as epigenetic influence, ancestral suffering, soul-level injury, past-life trauma and various other soul wounds are discussed. Up-to-date categorization of anxiety disorders is shared along with corresponding soul-related factors that may affect each concern.

No other author has illuminated the soul side of treating mental health concerns in this specific way. And no other has comprehensively addressed how the integration of body, mind and soul strategies are necessary to help a person feel whole again. While several authors have applied a general understanding of how the soul is related to psychology, none have offered a detailed approach to how it affects everyday life, our direct experience of anxiety or how to treat particular manifestations of the concern.

Part One in this book, **The History of Healing Anxiety,** explores the evolution of understanding and treating anxiety-related concerns, including the most recent categorization of disorders according to the standard manual used by mental health professionals in the United States. Traditional methods designed to treat the body and mind are reviewed to include most up-to-date methods and examples are provided for how some of these treatment protocols actually inhibit full healing when it comes to deeper aspects. *The Soul Health Model*™ is briefly explained to illustrate human factors within each "branch" of health that directly impact the experience of anxiety. Many soul-based aspects to anxiety are listed to prepare the reader for a deeper exploration of each later in the book. This section also explains my "*Three Levels of Healing*", which illuminates how the soul directly influences symptoms, thought processes and reactions of anxiety-related disorders as well as explains why body and mind approaches, alone, are not sufficient in treating this rapidly growing and pervasive condition.

Part Two, The Soul Side of Anxiety, more thoroughly describes *The Soul Health Model*™ as well as many additional human and soul factors that might underlie, exacerbate or inhibit healing from anxiety-related concerns. The model is then adapted to illustrate more directly how each "branch" of health may cause individuals to manifest anxiety-related symptoms from many common stressors within the human condition. Soul-related factors are more deeply described, along with examples in which they may manifest or present themselves in the most commonly known anxiety-based conditions. This section prepares readers for an exploration of soul-based factors that impact overall mental health and coping, but aren't taught in traditional forms of education.

The final section of this book, **Anxiety: The New Treatment Paradigm**, introduces a "whole soul experience" approach to treating anxiety-related disorders, while stressing the importance of attending to the soul as an essential part of healing. Suggestions for an enhanced conceptualization of anxiety-related disorders is included, along with potential assessment strategies and methods of integrating care. Both use a much wider and deeper lens for more complete understanding of the body, mind and soul aspects that impact this common condition. Suggestions for integration and accessing care from other professionals and modalities is explored, as well as cautions to exploring alternative strategies without professional expertise to guide the process.

How To Use This Book

Anxiety: Treating Body, Mind and Soul was written to expand and enhance your understanding of anxiety-related disorders whether you are struggling with anxiety yourself or if you are a practitioner attempting to more fully grasp the nature of these life-altering concerns. Although not all individuals will need or ascribe to this depth of treatment, it is helpful to appreciate that deeper origins of anxiety may exist beyond what is commonly known in contemporary treatment of these disorders.

As a practitioner, it is particularly important to know that nearly eighty-five percent (85%) of patients wish their providers integrated spirituality into the care they're offered, while less than ten percent (< 10%) ever do. Because of this lack of attention to what patients find important in their healing process, millions of individuals are already seeking guidance from various healers, shamans and other soul-healing professionals outside of current healthcare. Unless a practitioner is knowledgeable and open to enhanced methods of treatment, you may never know what your patient is doing outside of your traditional approach. It is time to integrate all aspects of a person's experience to improve both medical and mental healthcare. While treatment of the body and mind are necessary, it may not be enough to treat the whole soul in their experience.

While I would love to fully describe the various soul-healing theories and methods that may assist in the treatment of anxiety-related concerns, there aren't enough pages in a book to appropriately teach every approach. Instead, my intention here is to illustrate that the origin of some anxiety-based conditions may run deeper than traditional methods can reach. I also want to provide brief descriptions of soul-healing modalities that are available to supplement treatment of the most persistent concerns. Many suggestions for further learning about these modalities are provided throughout this book.

Most of all, I want to bridge a major gap between the body, mind and soul for both individuals who experience anxiety and for those who treat them. In an ideal world, a practitioner would understand and know how to address all three aspects when addressing a core concern. This is what early doctors attempted to do—one professional would attempt to treat an individual from an overall perspective. It is also essential to understand that three levels of healing are essential to help an individual feel whole (to be discussed in Part One of this book). However, as the field of medicine has become more specialized in how provision of care is provided, many interdisciplinary practitioners are now called upon to work on behalf of an individual patient.

The same is true for treating the soul; it takes a specialist to help a person find true "whole health". In this case, it takes someone who understands the nuances of this inner force and how it interacts with and affects a person's experience of anxiety within the human condition to make healing complete. While too few "soul specialists" exist, I intend to change that both by writing about many mental health conditions in *The Soul of Psychology* series and by providing specialized training to practitioners, coaches, educators and administrators who are interested in understanding the whole soul treatment of mental health concerns.

Admittedly, writing this book and others in the series has posed a challenge of finding the language to convey how to integrate the body, mind and soul into everyday practice. All aspects intersect to make a person complete, but the language about each is unfortunately quite separate. As are the methods and approaches. In recognizing this, I provide many metaphors to conceptualize and explain how each component of healing is essential in creating whole health. In doing so, I attempt to paint the picture of the soul in such a way that you can assimilate and embrace the concepts easily and deeply. As you will find later in this book, I use the term "soul health" to describe the experience of feeling balanced, whole and complete. Those who struggle with anxiety deserve to feel all of these.

The soul has been neglected far too long in the treatment of any medical or mental health concern. Since the inception of "modern" treatment of medical and mental health conditions, the soul has been progressively eliminated from the conceptualization of healing. For centuries, we have treated individuals from the outside in. It is now time to treat individuals from the inside out—it is time to elevate the soul back to its rightful place in mental health care. We can no longer separate the body and mind from the soul in the process of healing.

While anxiety is the fastest growing worldwide mental health concern, "good enough" management of symptoms is no longer adequate. ALL factors that affect those with anxiety-related disorders—physical, emotional **AND** soul-based—must be explored and addressed for true healing to occur.

PART ONE
THE HISTORY OF HEALING ANXIETY

You don't have a soul. You are a soul. You have a body.

C.S. LEWIS

CHAPTER ONE
SOUL ORIGINS OF ANXIETY

The cure of the part should not be attempted without the treatment of the whole. No attempt should be made to cure the body without the soul.

PLATO

The soul has been around far longer than modern medicine, psychology or any other scientific field. Yet, the most important part of who we are has been left out of healing care. As long ago as 400 BC, Greek philosopher, Socrates explored the importance of the "essence of who a person is", believing that it is immortal and eternal. Plato, his student, is first to posit that the soul was the source of life and mind, the force that animates every living being. Galen, a Greek philosopher, physician and surgeon explicitly took this idea further to describe in what part of the body the soul might exist. Finally, Hippocrates, who is said to be "the father of medicine" is the first physician to emphasize that this essence manifests in all disease conditions. The Hippocratic Oath, the most widely known doctrine in ancient medical texts, is primarily exercised by graduating physicians to "swear by a number of healing gods" to uphold specific ethical standards in the provision of care for whole healing of a person.

So, then, how is it that modern medical treatment completely ignores and dismisses what the field was first based upon—the very foundation upon which it was formed? How has the soul been ignored for so long? And how did the very essence of who we are get left out of healing?

Even before medicine was modernized, the first healers were always the spiritual leaders within the community, culture or tribe. When religion became formalized, these orders most often ministered to the sick, providing physical care but always with the assumption that the illness, condition or injury was only healable through a belief in God or some other sacred source. Regardless of how formal, cultural or internalized a spiritual basis was; all healers assumed that both the root cause and the ability to heal were related to the beliefs held by both those administering relief and those they served.

When thinking about the evolution of healthcare, the history of words is interesting as well. Although early Greek philosophers explored the idea of the soul very early on, the words "health" and "whole", now often used interchangeably, weren't documented until the twelfth century, A.D. The Old Norse use of the word "health" included "sacred or holy" in the definition, but after this, health and soul somehow became separate concepts.

The word "psychology" wasn't known until the year 1749, with the actual field born over one hundred years later (1879). Carl Jung, one of the founding fathers, established himself as a key player in the early 1900s, emphasizing that the soul—not the libido as Sigmund Freud had believed—drove all aspects of human experience. While establishing several of the foundational concepts of psychology that remain today, Jung was still somewhat dismissed by certain colleagues as a mystic because he explained how the spiritual aspects of an individual were closely intertwined with how the person responded to life. In his writings, he shared many of his own experiences including seeing the images of spirits, his understanding that astrological personalities weren't just thoughts of the occult and that his travel to various places around the world brought recognition of memories from the past that couldn't be explained by experiences in his current life alone. Jung was very much revered and honored by multiple international universities, but his work regarding the soul has been obscured since before his death in 1961. In his eighty-five years, he worked to understand and illuminate the importance of this vital force, but it is yet to be acknowledged as an essential feature in the understanding and treatment of mental health disorders.

How has the soul been forgotten? Because you can't measure the soul, you can only study and observe the experience of it. Even modern philosophers and religious spokespersons take an intellectualized approach to explaining self and soul, often missing the mark on acknowledging our deepest nature, especially when it comes to our psychological experience of life. Because traditional healthcare only seems to accept and support that which can be verified by instruments and calculation, the innermost self is overlooked altogether.

While most people practice various forms of spirituality and religion, somehow when it comes to treatment of the most common and pervasive concerns—both medical and mental—the soul is completely left out of the exam room. However, it is important to keep in mind that every monumental discovery first occurred through the process of observation. Why is the soul any different?

Until more people observe and appreciate the influence of the soul, anxiety and other mental and/or medical concerns will only be managed and not resolved or cured. It is time to resurrect the initial awareness that the soul is present in every symptom and illness humankind experiences.

The History of Anxiety

Stress has existed as long as humans have roamed the planet. The human condition is not an easy thing. However, anxiety likely formed over time. Many confuse the terms "stress" and "anxiety" and use the words interchangeably. Yet, it is important to distinguish these experiences to help you understand that one is a normal part of life and the other is something that disrupts or misaligns us at an abnormal and significantly unsettling level. The former may upset our life, while the latter deeply affects who we are.

Stress is defined as a state of mental or emotional strain or tension that results from adverse or demanding circumstances. We experience some level of it every day, though often not disruptive enough to warrant treatment or care by a professional. The experience of stress includes the *perception* that our external stressors are too much for the internal resources—or learned coping mechanisms—we might have available to us at the time. In other words, stress occurs when a real threat or fear exists, no matter how big or small.

Anxiety, however, is more specifically an actual diagnosable condition characterized by excessive worry, nervousness or apprehension about real **or** perceived threats, typically leading to some sort of avoidant behavior and is often accompanied by physical symptoms such as increased heart rate, muscle tension, perspiration and even difficulty swallowing. Anxiety, then, often occurs when a person is unsettled to the point that the essence of who they are is triggered at such a deep level that they are rendered helpless in particular situations. Anxiety-related reactions often occur even when the threat or fearful stimuli or event don't really exist. While stress is something everyone experiences, anxiety seems to become part of a person's identity and sense of self. It changes the essence and experience of who we are, not just how we behave.

While stress is a cognitive awareness characterized by stressful thoughts about a reality-based situation, anxiety is characterized by a greater mental **and** physical *experience* of either a real or imagined situation. This experience includes both excessive worry and rumination, paired with acute or chronic physical manifestations of the tension or anxiety-producing stimuli. Anxiety becomes closely associated with how we believe, act and respond in every moment, which indicates that something much deeper is at stake. It should also be noted that a person can experience anxious emotions that do not meet the criteria for an actual diagnosis of an anxiety disorder. This will become clear once you read about the formal diagnostic measures in later chapters.

As you can see, stress and anxiety are closely related, but fundamentally different manifestations within the human condition. You might also recognize that both the people who struggle and the practitioners who treat them can easily mistake one for the other. It is easy to get into the habit of treating anxiety, when in fact it is really the management of stress that needs the attention. Also, just because a person may not like or know how to manage the experience of psychological stress, it doesn't mean they should be treated medically; stress should not be considered a diagnosable disorder. In this case, the body may not require treatment, while the mind might greatly benefit from psychological care to learn stress-management and reduction techniques. Treatment regarding the soul is a whole different aspect to care that will be discussed throughout this book.

If this simple difference isn't confusing enough, think about early attempts to explain what happened when individuals showed what was thought to be anxious symptoms in ancient times. As early as 5000 BC, descriptions of something that sounded much like post-traumatic stress appeared in ancient Indian writings. It wasn't until early Greek writers like Hippocrates, Cicero and Seneca (around 400 BC) described people with anxious symptoms that this concern became an area of more direct focus. Even then, "hysteria", as coined by these early Greek physicians, was attributed to females because at the time it was thought that only women could experience reactions such as panic. These doctors thought the reactions were caused by the uterus, which they believed "wandered around the body blocking passages, obstructing breathing and causing disease" (originally posited by Plato and supported by many other philosophers at the time). It was also suggested that these reactions were caused by "female semen", which when stored in the body due to lack of sexual intercourse, would turn to poison and make women behave in "strange and high strung" manners. Having sex, then, was generally considered to be the cure. (As an aside, research now indicates that sex for some people can provide temporary relief from stress, but not decrease diagnosable anxiety. In fact, as someone who treats patients who have suffered from sexual trauma, I can accurately state that pressured or unwanted sexual activity to "treat" anxious reactions could have actually exacerbated anxiety in most of those individuals. Because women were often sexually mistreated and assaulted in earlier generations, I'm certain sex as a form of treatment for anxiety was not the answer, and in fact likely caused more problems.)

During the Renaissance period women were, again, thought to be the only ones prone to hysteria, mostly because they were often accused of being witches. Stressful thoughts or "premonitions" about bad things happening led people to react strongly, reinforcing that females were mostly afflicted with the condition. Uncanny awareness of potential tragedy—or women's intuition—was mistaken for a condition that would later be proven to affect both genders. Talking about anxiety-related symptoms or exhibiting physical symptoms that couldn't otherwise be explained were often "treated" with torture (Spain), execution (Britain) or burning at the stake (primarily in Scotland).

The Victorian age didn't do much better for women in terms of attributing anxiety-related conditions to the gender. Unusual or "hysterical" behaviors caused women to be deemed crazy and resulted in removal from home to be placed in asylums where heinous "treatments" took place, including electroshock therapy, immersive ice baths and, in the most severe cases, lobotomy (removal of parts of the brain). Likely, however, these "anxious reactions" resulted from other commonly held beliefs that women should be quieted from speaking their minds as it caused frustration and anger that were both unbecoming and unacceptable at the time. Women who were anything but calm and submissive were considered to be ill. Males, however, were encouraged to be raucous and to act out, while also releasing their frustrations through the intense physical activity of farming, building construction, etc. (More to follow on the importance of exercise and physical activity in the treatment of anxiety.) It wasn't ladylike or acceptable for women to do anything more than pour tea and host social gatherings, so any pent-up energy likely did contribute to more emotional reactions than men displayed.

It wasn't until the American Civil War that the experience of male soldiers helped to balance the gender gap of anxiety-related expression of concerns. Many soldiers were thought to suffer from what was called "irritable heart syndrome" which included heart palpitations and shortness of breath, symptoms now commonly related to both panic disorder and post-traumatic stress syndrome (which is no longer considered an anxiety disorder, but a stress-induced disorder—more on this recategorization later in this section). The condition was named "nerve weakness" and was treated with opium, ethyl alcohol and bromide salts. While up until this time, anxiety was seen solely as a female concern, this era offered more understanding that males could struggle from anxiety-related difficulties as well.

Interestingly, it was the Russians who first recognized the psychological nature of anxiety-related conditions when, after the 1904 war with Japan, they sent psychiatrists along with soldiers to treat them on the battlefield. Treatment included sedation by barbiturate to calm tensions among those afflicted. However, at the time, sterilization—a procedure to make a person unable to produce children—was also an adjunctive treatment in case the condition, once identified, could be passed to offspring. It is unclear whether this "innovative" approach was intended to actually assist soldiers or prevent the misunderstood spread of an uncontrollable and invasive medical concern.

It wasn't until the middle 1900's that modern techniques were created to manage the symptoms of anxiety. Muscle relaxation, exposure therapy and some talk therapies were introduced around this time. However, intensive shock treatment was still administered to prevent suicide by those who were at risk of killing themselves from extreme manifestations of anxiety. The 1980's brought the term "anxiety disorder" by way of more extensive observation of symptoms and precipitating factors. Around 1990 it was discovered that antidepressant-type drugs relieved the symptoms of anxiety when the research related to neurotransmitters such as dopamine and serotonin indicated a need for biochemical rebalancing. Now, pharmaceutical research is booming as the field attempts to find more formulas to treat the body aspect of the illness.

The Evolution of a Soul-Healing Specialist

My own understanding of mental health in general—particularly related to anxiety disorders—has undergone an evolution as well. When I look back at the history, I realize I started my training around the time that many conditions first became more clearly defined. In 1986 I enrolled in an Honors Psychology class as part of my high school education and after just a few weeks, I knew I was supposed to be a psychologist. I imagined many possibilities for the course of my career, but never in my early years did I think I would learn to incorporate the soul into the work I do. I was interested in spiritual concepts from a very young age, but because none of my training included an integration of medical, health and soul-based work; it didn't occur to me that these aspects were related.

While completing my doctoral education, a small group of students and a professor came together to discuss spirituality as part of mental health. Very little research was available at the time but it felt important to explore the topic. Later, I completed a post-doctoral fellowship in Family and Community Medicine where I also completed my Master of Science in Public Health degree. I focused my research on interviewing physicians regarding their beliefs and interest in addressing spiritual concerns in their work. I've always leaned toward qualitative methods of research because, to me, you gain so much more contextual knowledge than by quantitative measures alone. The richness of information I received inspired further inquiry and exploration.

After completing the fellowship, I accepted a position as the Director of Behavioral Science in Family and Community Medicine at Wake Forest University School of Medicine in North Carolina. While there, I used my knowledge about health and wellness to teach medical and nursing students, residents, physician assistants and various other students-in-training as well as with various clients and health-related patient groups. As a professor, I also received specialized training from the Mind-Body Medical Institute at Harvard University to incorporate strategies such as the Relaxation Response into work with clients. Although I was part of the first Complementary and Alternative Medicine committee on the WFU campus, spiritual inquiry was nowhere visible within the system. I left that role to enter private practice where I could more widely explore health and wellness concepts and integrate spirituality into my work. I greatly valued the opportunity to interact with many different health professionals but I needed to find a place where I could fully embrace bigger concepts that weren't part of typical medical structure.

Soon after entering private practice, I opened a holistic health center called *Branches Holistic Health and Wellness*, which offered psychotherapy, nutrition services and education, fitness training, movement therapy (Yoga, Tai Chi, Qigong, Nia), energy work (Reiki and Huna) therapeutic massage and body work (various forms of massage and Neural Touch techniques), meditation training and various classes, workshops, corporate events and personal retreats. I had eighteen employees, all from different fields. That multi-disciplinary experience helped to solidify the need to integrate both holistic and spiritual methods of healing into the work I do. It became clear that patients resolved their issues much more quickly and completely when various methods of healing came together to create whole health. I eventually closed that center to maintain my own life-balance, but also to learn more about holistic and spiritual health strategies, write books, teach continuing education workshops and provide retreats.

All the while, I continued to engage in and learn about multiple soul-healing strategies, including deeper meditation and visualization techniques, two forms of energetic healing, hypnotherapy, sound therapy, aromatherapy, past-life regression therapy, Akashic readings, Soul Realignment and more. I also created many of my own soul-healing methods to use with clients. As time went on, I began to see that many mental health concerns stem from wounds that are often untouchable by methods provided in traditional medical and mental healthcare. I realized that integrating traditional and holistic methods was the only approach that made sense. The deeper I dove into my own personal growth, spiritual beliefs and soul healing, the more I understood this approach could not be denied when addressing overall health for others.

We've come a very long way in understanding and managing anxiety, but traditional methods have a long way to go in overcoming more complicated and less understood aspects of the most common conditions. Too few people understand how the body, mind and soul are all responsible for the complete picture of mental health concerns, particularly when it comes to anxiety-related disorders.

With this book, all of that will change.

CHAPTER TWO

THE PSYCHE AND THE SOUL

Anxiety is a thin stream of fear trickling through the mind. If encouraged, it cuts a channel into which all other thoughts are drained.

ARTHUR SOMERS ROCHE

Before going much further, it is important to say that the word "soul" is not used in this book as a religious term; it simply explains the driving force within every living being on this planet. While this description of the soul is simple, the psyche is actually far more complicated to understand. However, because the psyche is more measurable and easier to categorize, we think we have a better handle on it, particularly with growing research and observation. The soul, though, is much harder to pin down since it currently isn't part of our everyday vocabulary and there's no way to put a label, number or statistical measure on it. We can't hook it up to a machine, ask it to fill out a questionnaire or place it under observation. Perhaps that is why no one talks about it or tries to fully define what it is.

What you will come to understand in reading this book and any other within the *Soul of Psychology Series*, is that it is not just the psyche that can be damaged, wounded or malfunction as a result of the challenging experiences of the human condition; the soul can suffer as well. Once a person comes to appreciate more about how the soul influences us and how to heal any wounds left on it by unsettling events, life becomes much easier. It directly improves when we practice soul-based healing.

While the soul is an invisible, unmeasurable force within us, it is the most important part of who we are. While initially illusive, it is actually quite tangible once a person knows how to acknowledge and access this energy within. The soul is the very *essence* of each individual and no two are the same. It is said that the human body has evolved about as much as it is going to but the soul has the infinite potential for growth—but only when it has been given the attention to be healthy and whole. As will be discussed in a later chapter, energy cannot die—it can only transform. It can either go on to expand and evolve or become stagnant, fractured or unbalanced depending on what the human condition has dealt each individual. As you will see in future chapters, our soul may require repair when treatments designed to address issues of the body and mind are not enough. But first, an explanation regarding the difference between the psyche and the soul is necessary to help you understand the importance of treating all components of whole-person health.

The Psyche and Anxiety

The psyche and the soul are often confused. In fact, these words are frequently used interchangeably. However, there is a fundamental difference. The psyche is the totality of the human mind, including the conscious and unconscious, whereas the soul is defined as the eternal energy—the unique essence within each of us—that drives all aspects of life. Overlap exists between the two, but they are distinct qualities of being human.

Carl Jung, the founder of analytic psychology, explained both the difference and the overlap through three levels he described that make humans whole: the conscious (ego personality), the personal unconscious (personal factors that influence our responses) and the collective unconscious (the generational accumulation of concepts and cultural "rules" or mindset that create certain core needs, fears or motivations). Each plays an important part in how we respond to the events in our lives, particularly when it comes to the experience of anxiety. Jung also taught that each played a part in the overall expression of an individual's soul.

According to Jung, the *conscious* aspect of the psyche is the part we show to others—it is what others see and is played out through the personality from which we interact. The *personal unconscious* is less obvious to others but is described to operate according to our insecurities, wounds and programmed influences from life experiences or past events. Jung believed these events initiated our first experience of anxiety because the way in which we react to stressors usually stems from previously impactful events. (Jung did not talk about past-life traumas as possible initiators, but you will hear more about this later in the book.) In contrast, the *collective unconscious* includes the generational accumulation of concepts and cultural "rules" or mindsets that define certain core needs, fears or motivations.

Our experience of the collective unconscious might be displayed through our group reactions to certain events or a seemingly inherent fear of animals such as snakes or the common uncertainty of what looms in the dark. (Current ideas about ancestral trauma might also apply.) According to Jungian theory, we can have an anxious personality (conscious mind), which might be triggered from reactions to past events (personal unconscious), while also having collective fear about something that has never directly impacted our life (collective unconscious).

When it comes to anxiety-related concerns, the *body* aspect might be displayed through anxious reactions that others can observe as a result of our internal discomfort (fidgetiness, perspiration, shortness of breath, agitation, etc.) as well as those less observable (heart palpitations, tightness in the chest, tingling in hands, etc.). These symptoms are often assessed when determining if a person struggles with an anxiety disorder. The facets of the *mind* may be identified through patterns of behavior that indicate a trigger to our emotional reactions from past wounds, trauma or fearful events or something that is feared to happen in the future. These facets are not immediately knowable to others, but are often explored during counseling, therapy or psychiatric service to assist in understanding and relieving physical symptoms.

Less known to many, in addition to a person's psyche becoming fractured or fragmented due to traumatic events, *soul* aspects can become damaged or wounded as well. Left to an untrained practitioner, an individual's symptoms related to the body and mind can persist and even worsen if deeper misalignments or injuries are left unattended. Soul aspects can also include reactions from the collective unconscious—discomfort and disturbance related to things a person might not even know are operating beneath the surface. This accounts for the growing awareness about ancestral wounds and generational programming. These aspects of anxiety are actually imprints on the soul that may cause us to react to experiences we've not had direct exposure to in the current life but is pre-programmed into our responses from previous generations.

Although the psyche is more related to a person's perceived personality and how they react in life, the soul is seen as the driving force behind all personality characteristics and is also the energetic force that drives individuals in all aspects of life—physical, psychological, social, interpersonal, intellectual/occupational, environmental, financial, sexual, spiritual and recreational as seen in *The Soul Health Model*™. These aspects of the human condition and their relation to anxiety will be further discussed in upcoming chapters. The fact is, there is something larger and deeper going on behind our personality or psyche that encompasses every aspect of our being, both conscious and unconscious. Much attention is currently being given to the study of consciousness and how this impacts everyday life. What scientists already know is that consciousness does not equal the psyche but precedes it. What soul-healing practitioners know is that the term "consciousness" is not synonymous with the word "soul". However, it is true that the more conscious an individual becomes, the more able they are to access and attend to their vital force. Conscious evolution, then, is a part of both soul healing and soul evolution. Both topics will be explored more fully in a later chapter in the book.

The Soul of Anxiety

The soul is commonly defined as the spiritual or immaterial part of a human being or animal that is said to be immortal. It lives on even after death. While each soul has its own identity, the collective of these identities, to Jung, plays a part in each person's life through the influence of the collective unconscious. Yet, each soul is unique and each has its own path to follow through this human condition. Simply put, the soul is our core, the light within. When this inner light misfires, burns irregularly or feels out of control, the human body that houses it experiences the physical symptoms of anxiety and the mind feels like it is running amok. Taking this into consideration, anxiety can be explained through a soul's inability to function smoothly due to wounds or injuries that contribute to an individual's overall experience in life. Because the manifestation of anxiety in many individuals seems to be unexplainable, it is important to consider that deeper imbalances or wounds may exist.

The soul is the center of everything that makes us human. It is the hub of all thoughts, behavior and motivation. It is a central operating system that runs deep within us. Whether we are aware of it or not, it is the driving force inside us that influences every aspect of our existence. It is the internal aspect that makes us want to survive even in the most dismal and desperate times. It is also the aspect of us that tells us what to do in the event of a crisis or emergency even when our thoughts become unclear. Somehow, our gut reactions—the automatic instinct of the soul—drive us to go on. It influences every breath of our existence, regardless of what might be commonly assumed in traditional treatment of any concern and, in this case, in the treatment of anxiety.

Like millions of other people, I've experienced anxiety of my own. While my disposition (both genetic and soul-based—more on this in later chapters) tends to lean toward depression, we know through research that anxiety is closely related. I have experienced both an occurrence of panic and occasional generalized anxiety symptoms (heart palpitations, shortness of breath, rumination and worrisome thoughts, etc.) but thankfully I knew these signs were related to what was misaligned in my life at the time. Deep down, I knew my human condition was out of balance. My soul—the essence of who I am—was alerting me to figure out a different way of doing life. If I hadn't known to hear and listen to my inner ally, I would have thought something was terribly wrong at a physical level. Instead, symptoms related to my mental health were the signs that something deeper needed attention.

The Physics of the Soul

You cannot understand the soul without understanding energy. Energy is defined as the property behind matter that causes motion or the ability of molecules to interact. However, the field of quantum physics takes energy to a higher level of understanding as it seeks to explain the building blocks of nature through the study of material, chemistry, biology and astronomy. We already know that energy is behind the development and expansion of every particle on the planet and throughout the universe, but no scientific field has fully pinpointed the unique force behind each living thing whether it be a tiny bug, a human, a star or even the universe itself. Science cannot explain the driving force or unique quality of each, but research does indicate that every separate entity or phenomenon is connected.

While there is no physical substance of the soul, the energy that is present in the billions of cells within a human body is animated by and connected to one invisible and unmeasurable driving force that makes us each a unique human. No two humans, including identical twins are completely alike when it comes to the soul, which means no two identical energetic human imprints or elements exist. While some authors have tried to explain the soul—the deepest aspect of who we are—through physics and the emerging field of consciousness, their intellectualized attempts to capture the true essence of this energy have failed. However, the soul can be described quite similarly to the most basic aspect of everything that exists—the atom, which is the smallest unit of energetic matter we know. Without atoms, no matter would matter at all.

Since everything in this world can be explained by energy, to some extent, the soul can be as well. For instance, scientists already know that atoms are the smallest building blocks of anything that exists and they know that the nucleus of each cell drives what each atom does. They also know that each cell within the human body (estimated to be between thirty and forty trillion cells) is made up of trillions of atoms. When it comes to healing the body from illness, scientists study how the energy or "behavior" of cells change as certain treatments or medications are administered. What researchers don't know is what exactly makes the smallest particle tick; they have no idea why the nucleus deep within each atom is programmed to be what it is or why those atoms act in the exact same way as all of the others that make up the whole of an individual. They simply know it is an amazingly intelligent micro aspect of what humans are.

The same is true for the soul. Just as the nucleus of each atom runs the show, the soul—or the nucleus of the essence of whom that individual truly is—directs all aspects of that person as well. We may not know why it does what it does, but we know what it does is beyond our comprehension.

Energy, the Soul and Anxiety

Scientists who study energy want to understand how it is organized. When it comes to the energy of the mind, in this case anxiety, the research becomes even more complex. In fact, groundbreaking studies regarding trauma, stress and neurobiology now lean toward applying what is called "Complexity Theory" to their models. Because complexity science represents a growing body of interdisciplinary knowledge about how things work, it applies perfectly to energy, the soul and mental health, particularly when it comes to the internal mechanisms that contribute to anxiety. The field emphasizes that to survive, a system "must be considered wholly in relation to how something evolves within the environment in which it operates". To survive, the system—in this case a human—must adapt in order to evolve. Therefore, the integration of knowledge across disciplines and the emergence of new concepts, tools and vocabulary are essential. This integration is the only way to develop important insights in the full treatment of anxiety and other mental health disorders.

While complexity theory applied to mental health concerns is revolutionary and growing, it still leaves out the soul. Most formal education related to anxiety disorders focuses on the body—the physical and/or genetic aspects that predispose a person to anxious responses and the mind—the cognitive or psychological patterns or characteristics that contribute to the manifestation of these disorders. Until now, no one yet has offered an explanation for what happens beyond the body and mind to cause distress.

Suffice it to say, the experience of anxiety can be described as evidence of a misalignment of energy deep within an individual's overall system. It is the misalignment or misfiring of energetic impulses within the body that cause an individual to feel uncomfortable, either physically or emotionally. These surges indicate that something is wrong and can be expressed through worry, panic and unsubstantiated reasons for many types of fear. This energetic malfunction can either present as a constant hum of discomfort or as a periodic flare or rush. When it comes to the soul running the show, the deepest energy within a human being can be fractured, fragmented or wounded in such a way that it causes the human experience of anxiety—the surges or flares that are currently only seen as body or mind-based reactions. However, it is time to accept and understand that these episodes may be related to the internal operating system of the individual—the *soul*—attempting to alert the holder that something deeper is misaligned, wounded or broken.

With regard to the panic reaction I experienced many years ago, I knew right away that something within me had short-circuited or misfired—my energetic system was trying to get my attention. At the time, I was in an unhealthy marriage, one that included much deceit. My mind was constantly on alert to identify when my husband was telling the truth. In the beginning, he was particularly good at convincing me I had been mistaken, but my inner truth began to tell me otherwise. At the point I experienced panic, I realized I needed to leave the marriage. My soul was telling me nothing would change and that I needed to get out.

Many years later when my mother's health declined, I began to experience heart palpitations and tightness in my chest. Although I expected stress to be part of the experience as she approached death, I didn't expect the intensity that came with challenging family dynamics at the time. Because I lived many states away, I traveled home often and sometimes because of urgent needs or requests. As a self-employed individual, my financial situation became a concern since I don't get sick leave or receive a salary, not to mention the thousands of dollars I spent on travel to get home. I also had an elderly dog that was suffering from cancer and felt the daily responsibility to maintain support for a very full load of clients. Many aspects of my life felt stretched beyond limits and my energetic system, once again, showed me that things were severely out of balance. All of this subsided a few months after her death when I could refocus my efforts on taking care of just me. I did see a cardiologist to assure that everything was okay and she confirmed that I was fine on a physical level. I haven't experienced the palpitations since. (Additional soul-based factors of anxiety will be discussed later in this book.)

Being a soul-healing specialist, I explored the many deeper origins of my discomfort that could be contributing to my anxious reactions. In addition to obvious life stressors, I realized some past-life circumstances involving family members were playing a significant part in the current discomfort. I also became aware of what is called "karmic energy" that was shifting with my mother's death and also through life lessons that were being presented to me throughout that time. Without knowing these layers of my experience were present, I would have become immensely concerned about my body and mind reactions. However, it was my soul that needed attention.

Unfortunately, most current treatments only target body and mind aspects of this anxiety; very few people know to look deeper. These approaches may help to manage some of the symptoms, but rarely do they cure the core issue. Flare-ups can continue even when treating the body and mind in traditional ways. If the soul is left unattended as part of whole health treatment of an individual, the person will be left feeling far less than complete.

In my own healing, I knew to attend to the body through exercise, good nutrition and consistent sleep as well as attention to the mind in talking through my concerns, journaling and airing out my thoughts. On a soul level, I knew the most healing would occur when I addressed and recovered from the soul wounds that existed both in the past and during and after my mother's passing. I recovered very quickly as a result of attending to my inner self and all symptoms of my anxiety dissolved. I've had no physical or emotional symptoms since and my soul is at peace.

While there is often a biological or psychological component behind the experience of anxiety, it is often the soul that needs attention. The combination of treatment for body, mind and soul is essential in a whole soul healing process.

CHAPTER THREE

THE EVOLUTION OF MODERN ANXIETY

No excellent soul is exempt from a mixture of madness.
ARISTOTLE

Anxiety-related reactions have existed since the beginning of humankind. However, the history and research associated with anxiety as a notable condition is actually rather new and changes all the time. While those who experience it know it is a very real, deep and visceral experience, many, including healthcare providers who treat them, know little about the history of how this set of concerns came to be what they are today. As mentioned in the introduction of this book, the understanding of mental health conditions originated with the soul in mind, but very few acknowledge this aspect currently. That is all about to change.

Ancient Origins of Anxiety

Many ancient physicians, scientists and philosophers have written about anxious reactions and several included the soul in their work. As early as the 350s BC, Aristotle acknowledged the impact of intense fear, noting that it was the opposite of confidence, attributing most challenges to heat in the body. He believed that fear made the body cold and led to physical symptoms such as trembling, sweating and urinating as part of a fearful experience. He wrote about an imbalance of the inner self and what this does to both a person's health and what we would now call well-being.

Greek philosopher Epicurus (341 to 270 BC), literally mentions the soul as he described his theory about anxiety. He was the first to explain the world through the idea of atoms (discussed in the previous chapter). Regarding anxiety, he believed that the misconfiguration of these tiny particles led to unbalanced "irreducibles, causing the body, mind and soul to experience distress". When out of balance, fearful thoughts and acts could become painful and thus work against the body. He even said that to adopt his atomic viewpoint would "take people's fear away from the power of the gods." Epicurus's theory of "misalignment" is similar to what I discuss in the chapter about *The Soul Health Model*™, which presents a practical understanding of the concept of needing to realign our lives to create more balance and ease.

Galen (129 to 216 CE), a Greek physician and philosopher, ascribed to the balance of opposites as a way to explain the uncomfortable emergence of thoughts and feelings. Like

Aristotle and Epicurus, he believed that the experience of intense discomfort and worrisome thoughts came from extreme imbalances and felt that trembling resulted from bearing too heavy of an emotional burden, which is not far off from current views of anxiety. Galen was also fascinated with the idea of the soul and even tried to map its physical location in the body according to his theory that certain organs must be imbalanced to cause *dis*-ease. Of course, no actual location exists, but his theory at least gave attention to the deep powers of the human spirit.

As mentioned in the introduction, Hippocrates (460-375 BC), the father of medicine, posited that the soul exists in every physical illness. In his time, mental disturbance was thought to stem from bodily concerns alone and a separate understanding of anxiety or other mental disorders wasn't mentioned until those after him shared their observations. However, he documented a man's extreme terror when hearing flute music, which would now be considered a phobia. According to his observations, the music seemed to be tolerable for the patient during the day, but during the night the man's negative reactions were substantial. He associated his intense fear with something unseen, but he definitely experienced it at a deep level. Although Hippocrates would have attributed this to something physical, even he knew that something deep within the patient caused him to pair music with the dark, thus creating his most dreaded fear. The man reported no previous traumatic event that would cause such an association and it was attributed to damage to the vital force within.

Contemporary Anxiety

The American Psychiatric Association published the first edition of the Diagnostic and Statistical Manual of Mental Disorders (DSM) in 1952, which marked the formal categorization of mental disorders of any type. This manual was initially presented as a 32-page spiral-bound pamphlet that contained information about 106 diagnoses, the vast majority stemming from origins which were physical in nature (brain abnormality, etc.). Now, the DSM-5-TR (Text Revision), contains 1120 pages that define approximately 300 conditions in far more detail, many of which are subsets of the about seventy-five primary disorders. The DSM is now considered the diagnostic "bible" of the mental health world and the majority of medical and mental health practitioners refer to this as the gold standard of any emotional concern.

Sadly, no edition includes or even alludes to the soul as an aspect to be considered in either conceptualization or treatment of mental health disorders. While not mainstream, only spiritual or soul-healing practitioners know the influence of the soul in the treatment of whole person health. This is unfortunate since the DSM is supposed to have all the answers.

Understanding the progression of "modern anxiety" will help to appreciate that there is still much to learn about the concern.

DSM-I: The first edition of DSM-I (1952) didn't include anxiety as a disorder, classifying it only as a reaction to stressful stimuli or events.

DSM-II: By 1968, the DSM added a category titled "Anxiety neurosis," characterizing the condition as an "over-concern extending to panic and frequently associated with somatic symptoms."

DSM-III: In 1980, the DSM-III distinguished different kinds of anxiety by including phobic disorders (agoraphobia with or without panic attacks and social phobia), anxiety states such as panic disorder, generalized anxiety disorder (GAD), obsessive-compulsive disorder (OCD) and post-traumatic stress disorder (PTSD). The DSM added anxiety disorders of childhood as well (separation anxiety disorder, avoidant disorder and overanxious disorder).

DSM-IV: In 1994, the DSM-IV divided anxiety disorders into five primary categories: GAD, OCD, panic disorders, PTSD and social anxiety, with all other categories accounted for within these.

DSM-IV-TR (Text Revision): By 2000, the categories for anxiety included panic disorder (with or without agoraphobia (fear of open spaces), agoraphobia (with or without a history of panic disorder), specific phobias, social phobia, OCD, PTSD and GAD.

DSM-V: A major overhaul occurred with the publication of the DSM-V in 2013. At this point, the chapter on anxiety no longer included OCD or PTSD, having categorized them as obsessive reactive or trauma and stressor-related reactions (respectively) rather than including them as anxiety disorders in general. It made other changes to terminology for phobias and social anxiety. It added separation anxiety and selective mutism to the anxiety disorder category, since a primary feature is an anxiety-related response.

DSM-V-TR (Text Revision): The authors further re-categorized the DSM-V-TR (Text Revision) and published it in March 2022. Anxiety disorders now include separation anxiety disorder, selective mutism, specific phobias, social anxiety disorder, panic disorder, agoraphobia, GAD and substance/medication-induced anxiety disorder. Therefore, these will be the focus of the current book.

As you can see, the very idea of anxiety has undergone much debate and reconceptualization. The only thing still missing is the soul.

Soul Aspects of Currently Acknowledged Anxiety Disorders

I describe here all currently categorized anxiety disorders in general medically defined terms. Most people will readily recognize some, but a few are less known by the mass public. The soul-based aspects of these conditions will be more fully explored in future chapters but here I provide a few common associations. Later in the book, I provide much more information about possible soul-related factors of anxiety to help readers understand how influences such as past-life trauma, epigenetic influence, ancestral trauma and situations which may have created soul injury in both the current life or past ones may impact an individual today. For now, I list a few examples to begin expanding your conceptualization and understanding of common anxiety-related concerns.

Separation Anxiety Disorder

Separation anxiety is a condition in which an inordinate level of anxiety is experienced by an individual upon separation from others in which the party has formed a close emotional attachment. Three of the following must be experienced for a formal diagnosis to be made:

- Repeated intense anxiety when anticipating or experiencing separation from home or significant others
- Incessant rumination over the prospect of loss of or harm to the attachment figure
- Incessant worry about an adverse event occurring to oneself that results in separation from the attachment figure
- Chronic refusal or unwillingness to venture away from home due to fear of separation
- Chronic and significant anxiety about being left alone and separated from the attachment figure
- Refusal or unwillingness to sleep away from home while separated from attachment figures
- Recurring nightmares about separation
- Recurring complaints of physical ailments when anticipating or experiencing separation

The fear behavior must be present for at least four weeks, cause significant distress or impairment and is not better explained by another mental disorder.

Possible Soul-Based Causes of Separation Anxiety:

The following are examples of soul-based origins that are linked to current-life experiences of separation anxiety.

- Past-life trauma in which an individual experienced a tragic loss of a non-specific loved
- one (or more than one loved one) that influences anxiety reactions in this lifetime
- Past-life trauma in which an individual lost a particular attachment figure who is also present in this lifetime (such as a partner, spouse or family member), which activates anxiety reactions in this lifetime
- Abandonment concerns that are tied to tragic loss of family of origin or other soul-related group members in current or past lives (neglect, adoption, genocide, war, pandemics, etc.), which triggers anxiety reactions
- Ancestral scaring from tragic events that the current soul energetically carries (holocaust, cultural tragedies, historical natural disasters, etc.), which influences reactivity to certain anxiety-provoking situations

Selective Mutism

Selective mutism is a condition in which an individual displays a reticence to speak in situations where speaking is typically expected (social, educational or vocational aspects of life). This silence or difficulty communicating must last at least one month and is not due to difficulties with vocabulary or language. It can appear as if the person is ignoring signals or just refusing to speak, but the individual simply cannot form words when in certain situations.

- Consistent failure to speak in specific social situations despite speaking in others
- Disturbance interferes with educational or occupational achievement
- Failing to speak is not attributable to a lack of knowledge or, or comfort with the spoken language of the social situation
- The disturbance is not better explained by a communication disorder and does not occur in relation to another disorder

Possible Soul-Based Causes of Selective Mutism:

Selective mutism is a rare manifestation of anxiety, with several possible soul-based origins. Some include:

- Current or past-life trauma in which a particular individual is inhibited in speaking freely in this lifetime. This could stem from being beaten or tortured in a past life, possibly by a soul who is present in this lifetime as well.
- Past-life trauma in which the same soul beat or tortured an individual in a situation similar to one in the current lifetime (not necessarily in another lifetime), influencing anxious responses to similar events

- Ancestral trauma in which an individual, in the present, emotionally carries generational wounds which influence their reaction to particular triggering events
- Energetic blockage in throat chakra from trauma in this or previous lifetime(s), an energetic manifestation that affects the ability to speak freely
- Misalignment of current situation with an individual's current soul/life mission and ability to speak his or her truth

Specific Phobias

A specific phobia relates to a disproportionate fearful response to a specific object or situation that is almost immediately elicited by the presence of the phobic object or situation or the individual actively avoids the phobia-producing entity or tolerates it with immense anxiety.

- Marked fear or anxiety about a specific object or situation
- The phobic object or situation always provokes intense and immediate fear or anxiety
- The phobic object or situation is actively avoided or endured with intense fear or anxiety
- The fear or anxiety is out of proportion to the actual danger posed

Currently, over 500 known phobias exist, most extremely rare. The experience of a phobia must be present for six months or more, cause significant emotional distress, and is not better explained by symptoms of another disorder. Experts categorize most phobic conditions as fears of Animals (spiders, insects, dogs), Natural Environments (heights, storms, water), Blood-Injection-Injury (needles, invasive medical procedures), Situational (airplanes, elevators, enclosed places), or Other (choking, vomiting, loud sounds or costumed characters).

Possible Soul-Based Causes of Specific Phobias:

Past-life traumas can be linked to many unexplained phobic reactions in this lifetime. Also, the fact that most phobias are extremely rare lends some significance to soul-based influences when nothing in a patient's current lifetime can explain these disturbances and associations. Here are some examples:

- In the current lifetime, past-life traumatic events involving animals such as cultures being hunted by dogs or surrounded by insects like locusts and flies manifest

- Past-life events related to floods, drowning, or falling from high places which cause anxious reactions

- Past-life traumatic experiences related to airplanes, trains, bridges (war and other tragedies), which cause unexplained fear of these aspects of travel in this lifetime

- Health-related anxiety that stems from illness/injury in past lives (plagues, pandemics, injury or other historical health-related events), causing inordinate stress related to health in this lifetime

- Epigenetic influences/ancestral trauma (torture using certain instruments, invasive medical procedures) that unknowingly impact individuals and their reactions to certain stimuli

SOCIAL ANXIETY DISORDER

Social anxiety is described as a condition in which a person experiences inordinate fear in situations that might subject them to evaluation by others (during meetings, engaging in conversations with unfamiliar parties, being observed or giving speeches or presentations). The individual is greatly concerned that they may behave in inappropriate or unacceptable ways that would be negatively construed (leading to rejection, embarrassment, ridicule or being offended). Therefore, the person avoids social situations or endures them with enormous anxiety.

- Marked fear or anxiety about one or more social situations in which the individual perceives scrutiny by others

- The individual fears that his or her actions or anxiety symptoms will be negatively evaluated by others

- The social situations almost always provide fear or anxiety

- Individuals experience intense fear or anxiety when avoiding or enduring the social situations
- The fear or anxiety is out of proportion to the actual threat posed by the social situation

Symptoms of social anxiety must be present for six months or more, cause significant distress or impairment, must not be attributable to the physiological effects of a substance or medication, are not better explained by the symptoms of another mental disorder and be identified as separate from another medical condition that could cause fear or anxiety (Parkinson's disease, disfigurement from an injury, etc.).

Possible Soul-Based Causes of Social Anxiety Disorder:

Social anxiety has many possible soul-related aspects, many of which are related to interpersonally based soul wounds present from past lives. Some include:

- Public ridicule or humiliation in this lifetime or previous lives that cause an individual to be unusually anxious in this lifetime
- The individual's past-life trauma involved a fear of persecution or actual experiences of persecution, resulting in an immediate fear of it in this lifetime
- Epigenetic influence/ancestral trauma, in which previous generations experienced ridicule, humiliation or persecution, influencing the individual to respond anxiously in this lifetime

- Soul composition, or the way in which a soul was energetically created, can be related to why and how a person experiences discomfort in interacting with others in this lifetime

Panic Disorder

Repeated panic attacks, depicted as sudden, unexpected, intense fear responses during which anxiety rapidly escalates within minutes, is another common anxiety-related concern. The individual must experience at least four of the following:

- Rapid heartbeat
- Sweating
- Shaking
- Shortness of breath
- Choking sensation
- Chest pain/discomfort
- Nausea or gastrointestinal distress
- Vertigo/sensation of loss of balance or feeling faint and lightheaded
- Sensations of heat or cold
- Paresthesias (sensation of tingling or prickling somewhere in the body, usually the hands or feet)
- Derealization (feeling detached from thoughts, feelings and body)

- Fear of losing emotional control
- Fear of dying

After experiencing at least one panic attack, there has been at least one month of one or both of the following:

- Chronic worry about experiencing an additional panic attack (and their possible consequences)
- Marked effort to engage in behaviors to avoid the panic
- Other maladaptive behavior change may be present to attempt to compensate for fearful reactions

Symptoms must not be attributable to physiological effects of a substance or medication and must not be explained by another mental disorder. However, some cultural-specific symptoms should not account for one of the four required symptoms.

Possible Soul-Based Causes of Panic Disorder:

It is not unusual for panic disorders to emerge without a particular initiating event or identifiable cause. Sometimes soul-based wounds can emerge from unresolved issues in past lives, severe past-life trauma that has created a programmed sensitivity to react, or stimuli that triggers unconscious wounding from the past. Some examples are:

- General past-life reactions which mimic or mirror experiences in current life without a specific cause in this lifetime

- Past-life trauma related to specific events or interactions that are unresolved, causing a person to attribute unknown anxious meaning to certain events

- Energetic malfunction that originated from past-life trauma (general misfiring of an individual's energetic system which indicates soul fracturing from previous life experiences)

- Misalignment of an individual's energetic blueprint with current life situations and/or their life purpose or mission (i.e., energetic system doesn't align with or match earthly or human energies or is misaligned with overall soul's energetic structure)

Agoraphobia

Someone who experiences agoraphobia has significant anxiety about at least two of the following scenarios:

- Using public transportation
- Being in open spaces
- Being in enclosed spaces
- Being in a crowd
- Being alone outside one's home
- The individual fears or avoids these situations because escape might be difficult
- The situations always provoke fear or anxiety

- The individual requires the presence of a companion in anxiety-provoking situations
- The fear or anxiety is disproportionate to the actual danger

The above listed scenarios are avoided due to fear of being trapped or fear of experiencing symptoms of panic. Agoraphobic scenarios almost always elicit distress and anxiety, require the individual be accompanied, or are endured while experiencing intense fear. An individual must experience symptoms for at least six months and the symptoms cause significant distress or disturbance in their lives. All other medical and mental health conditions must be ruled out to account for a diagnosis of Agoraphobia.

Possible Soul-Based Causes of Agoraphobia:

Agoraphobia has many past-life and soul-based origins that could impact an individual's experience of anxiety:

- Past-life soul wounds that stem from intensely vulnerable or terrifying situations (death in gas chambers during the Holocaust, imprisonment, running from soldiers or enemies, etc.) that cause fear of either open or closed spaces
- Abandonment in large spaces due to sudden past-life events (sudden bombings during previous wars, entrapment in structures due to natural disasters) that left them alone, without the care of loved ones

- In-vitro trauma from pre-birth experiences (fetal distress, abuse of mother while pregnant, emotional/mental rejection of the fetus by the mother, etc.)
- Past-life trauma related to forced abandonment of home (invasions, war, etc.), causing person to fear leaving their comfortable environment

Generalized Anxiety Disorder (GAD)

Those who experience an inordinate level of worry about a variety of scenarios are considered having generalized anxiety disorder (GAD). The individual finds it difficult to not ruminate about worrisome scenarios, which may or may not be reasonable concerns for others. Three of the following symptoms must be present (with at least one lasting a minimum of six months) for a formal diagnosis:

- Agitation/Restlessness
- Tiredness
- Difficulty focusing or concentrating
- Irritability
- Muscular tension
- Difficulty sleeping

As with all other disorders, GAD must impair function for at least six months and not be attributable to the physiological effects of a substance or medication, or better explained by another mental health condition.

Possible Soul-Based Causes of Generalized Anxiety Disorder (GAD):

Many soul-based factors can contribute to the experience of generalized anxiety in individuals. Some include:

- Reactions related to the individual's astrological personality (example: astrological chart that indicates particular life lessons in this lifetime) that influence how an individual copes in day-to-day life

- Unresolved issues from past lives that include financial concerns from extreme poverty, food anxiety related to famine or hunger or general insecurity stemming from past-life trauma

- Life- or soul lessons that are part of the person's overall life path that they must overcome as part of their soul's evolution

- Ancestral fears that the individual has carried into this lifetime from the experiences of previous generations

SUBSTANCE/MEDICATION-INDUCED ANXIETY DISORDER

Panic attacks or anxiety can occur as a result of substance intoxication or withdrawal or following exposure to medication when either is capable of initiating severe anxiety.

Two criteria must be present:

- The symptoms of panic develop during or soon after substance intoxication or withdrawal or after the exposure to or withdrawal from a medication, and

- The substance/medication is capable of producing the symptoms of panic

As with all other disorders, this Substance/Medication-Induced Anxiety Disorder must rule out all other mental health disorders.

Possible Soul-Based Causes of Substance/Medication-Induced Anxiety Disorder:

While substance/medication-induced anxiety disorder is a somewhat newly categorized and defined condition, it is possible that some soul-based influences affect a person's experience. Most substance/medication reactions do seem to be primarily biologically based, however, in some circumstances it is possible that soul-based issues might contribute to a person's anxiety reaction:

- An individual's panic may be related to a severe reaction they had to medical treatments in previous lives, resulting in their reaction in this lifetime
- Anomalies in the individual's energetic system that interfere with the ability to process certain medications—could be related to a physical manifestation of past-life trauma

I listed just a few examples of ways soul-based causes could play a part in each DSM category of anxiety disorders; however, there are many more possibilities to consider. While you may not have thought about or been exposed to some concepts noted above, many of them probably made sense or resonated for you as you read along. Many of my clients, including those who are healthcare providers themselves, have found healing and peace as they consider the possibilities of soul-based origins of anxiety and other mental health disorders. Most have told me these explanations are the first that made sense in their many years of trying to overcome their persistent concerns. If you are a healthcare or mental health professional, keep in mind that you were likely only taught either a body or mind-based approach to treating those you serve. The information and concepts in this book might help you understand what has been missing when trying to address tough-to-treat issues.

The next chapter will provide more insight into the current approach to treating anxiety from a physiological standpoint. Because this book emphasizes the complexity of body, mind and soul aspects of this condition, an integration of treatment modalities that addresses all factors is most optimal as part of restoring whole person health. A reminder of body-based treatments that are already available will help you see how it is only part of the picture when treating anxiety-related concerns.

CHAPTER FOUR

TREATING THE BODY AND MODERN ANXIETY

We are souls dressed up in sacred biochemical garments and our bodies are the instruments through which our souls play their music.
ALBERT EINSTEIN

According to medical research, the exact cause of anxiety is still not known. Scientists have been able to link anxiety to many factors including changes in brain chemicals and its functioning, environmental stress, family history and stressful or traumatic life events, but they haven't been able to isolate the actual source. Several medical conditions have also been shown to trigger anxious reactions (heart issues, diabetes, thyroid problems, respiratory disorders, chronic pain, withdrawal from alcohol and other substances, and rare tumors that produce certain fight-or-flight hormones). But again, no direct answer exists.

As mentioned in a previous chapter, Complexity Theory is now being applied to many research-based dilemmas, mental health concerns being some of them. The Santa Fe Institute, an independently run education and research center, was founded in 1984 to study the complexity of certain systems and phenomena that have yet to be answered by scientific exploration. The institute emphasizes the importance of interdisciplinary research and collaborates with various universities, experts, research institutes and government agencies to answer the toughest questions of how things work. While researchers there are making strides in understanding the complex nature of the body and mind related to mental health and neurobiological phenomena, still no mention is made of the soul as a contributing factor in how an individual feels or behaves. Because the soul is the very essence of whom a person is, it makes sense to explore this vital force further.

The philosopher Plato said, "In order for man to succeed in life, God provided him with two means, education and physical activity. Not separately, one for the soul and the other for the body, but for the two together. With these two means, men can attain perfection." While treating the body alone will not help an individual heal from anxiety, it is one part of treating the whole soul experience.

Treating the Body for Anxiety Relief

Traditional treatment of anxiety focuses primarily on the body and mind of the individual. The research is growing regarding the efficacy of natural methods, medication and psychological intervention. However, it is generally recommended that those who suffer with anxiety receive treatment that includes all of these for best results. While natural methods such as exercise, meditation and other mind/body-balancing strategies are immensely helpful, most traditionally trained practitioners focus on medication and psychotherapy as the primary treatment protocol. Between 70 and 90% of people who included natural, medical and psychological methods as part of their treatment strategy report significant improvement in the management of symptoms. Even then, no one reports complete resolution. Something else is playing a part.

Anxiety is generally treated through four primary methods: medication, psychotherapy, alternative treatments and Transcranial Magnetic Stimulation (TMS). Because information regarding these forms of treatment is readily available, only a brief summary will be provided here. Psychotherapy will be discussed in the next chapter about treating the mind. But first, it is important to share the most effective method of managing symptoms for almost all mental health concerns related to the body: exercise. Although not considered an actual treatment, physical activity should be considered as part of any approach to whole person care.

Physical Activity

Exercise is not natural, but physical activity is. Cavemen and cavewomen didn't stop everything to go to the gym; their lives just kept them active. We will never know if people of that time experienced anxiety beyond expected levels of stress but we do know that the less physically active societies have become, the more anxiety they experience. Also, keeping soul health in mind, the longer a person lives and the more lifetimes they experience, the greater the chance a person has of accumulating deep injury that could impact the essence of who they are as they think, feel and act throughout their human condition. However, physical activity remains the most natural way to manage symptoms of most mental health concerns.

In 2010, a national news story announced that an unexpected treatment for anxiety and depression had been found, emphasizing that it was free and had no major side effects. The treatment was exercise. Although unconventional at the time, study after study shows that regular and moderate physical activity remains the most effective manager of most mental health conditions, particularly those that are anxiety-related. Not only does exercise help to manage anxiety and depression, it helps equally as well as medication. Research is also clear that those who exercise regularly tend to avert relapse of intense anxiety symptoms. In addition, cardiovascular activity tends to prevent anxiety and depression in those who aren't genetically predisposed. In other words, it can do very little wrong in helping and in fact, it does everything right in relieving symptoms and minimizing risk.

While physical activity does not treat the cause of anxiety, it does have many anxiety-reducing benefits. From a body perspective, physiological changes occur by raising levels of several neurotransmitters in the brain that are known to reduce anxiety: serotonin, norepinephrine, dopamine and endorphins. When these brain chemicals are increased through physical activity, side effects are non-existent and the positive effects tend to sustain.

Those who struggle with chronic anxiety are recommended to engage in moderate to strenuous physical activity on a regular basis to alleviate symptoms. This generally means an individual should participate in activity that elevates the heart rate for at least thirty minutes daily, although longer periods of exercise done less frequently also show a positive response for generalized anxiety (GAD). Regular walking or jogging (approximately four miles three times a week) can also reduce severity and frequency of panic attacks. This means that just an hour of moderate exercise three times a week can significantly reduce most symptoms that cause emotional discomfort.

While regular and moderate exercise are recommended, The Anxiety and Depression Association of America notes that even five minutes of aerobic exercise can begin to stimulate anti-anxiety effects and that a ten-minute brisk walk can provide several hours of relief. In 2018, the U.S. Department of Health and Human Services listed decreased anxiety as one of the most positive benefits of physical activity. No matter how you look at it, exercise is a top choice for decreasing anxious symptoms.

Related to my own management of anxiety throughout life, I realized during graduate school that exercise was a primary method of managing symptoms. In an earlier chapter I mentioned a time when anxiety was high due to my experience of an unhealthy marriage. In the midst of distress one evening, I found myself unable to focus on my studies. Between the stresses of being a graduate student and the challenging marriage, I just couldn't concentrate. I knew in that moment I had to release some tension, so I went to the student gym. It was mid evening, a time when I didn't typically work out; however, I somehow knew I had no other choice. I did my typical fifteen or so minutes on the Stairmaster—a fairly intense exercise, but it didn't do the trick. I transferred to the treadmill and started my typical fast-paced walk. Unfortunately, I could tell this wouldn't be enough either. I decided to crank up the pace and ran, something I was unaccustomed to doing.

Within about five minutes I could tell something was changing so I continued to jog along the stationary track. After a few more minutes, I literally felt something within me release like a valve—an instant lessening of my distress. I continued to run for several more minutes, just to be sure the feeling would sustain. I was able to return home, resume my studies and get a good night's sleep. From that moment on, I understood first-hand the therapeutic value to exercise in both the prevention and management of both stress and anxiety. I still work out almost daily as a result.

While the research continually reinforces the notion that physical activity is the best natural "medicine" for anxiety, I have personal proof to share each time a client presents with anxious concerns.

Medication

Biological management of anxiety has been the primary approach to treatment by medical professionals for several years. While medication alone is not recommended for the treatment of anxiety or most other mental health conditions, it can be helpful in managing symptoms, especially for those who don't exercise on a regular basis.

Several medications exist to relieve anxious symptoms, depending on the type of disorder an individual has. Four types of medications are generally used to treat anxiety:

Selective Serotonin Reuptake Inhibitors (SSRIs)

SSRIs provide relief by blocking reabsorption, or reuptake, of serotonin in the brain. This leaves more serotonin available, which improves the mood of the anxious individual. They are considered effective in the treatment of all anxiety disorders, but those who suffer from obsessive-compulsive disorder (OCD) generally need higher doses.

Serotonin-Norepinephrine Reuptake Inhibitors (SNRIs)

SNRIs provide dual action by increasing the levels of serotonin while inhibiting the reabsorption into brain cells. These medications are also considered effective for most anxiety disorders, but SSRIs are still considered more effective for people diagnosed with OCD.

Benzodiazepines

These types of drugs are generally used for short-term management of anxiety symptoms, although they are often used as an "add on" to treatment for people who have tough-to-treat or resistant anxiety symptoms. Use of benzodiazepines may lead to tolerance and dependence and should be closely monitored. These medications are not recommended for use by those who have post-traumatic stress disorder (PTSD).

Tricyclic Antidepressants

Tricyclic antidepressants are among the earliest antidepressants developed and while effective, they have generally been replaced by SSRIs and SNRIs. They are designed to assist in changing brain chemistry by blocking the reabsorption of both serotonin and norepinephrine, increasing these neurotransmitters in the brain. Although these drugs can be effective in some anxiety disorders, they can cause significant side effects and are often avoided as first choice for treatment. Social anxiety does not show positive results with this medication.

Note: Bioavailability is something to consider when taking psychotropic medications. This term refers to the proportion of a drug or substance that enters the circulation and is able to have an active effect when introduced into the body. While many holistic practitioners address these issues, traditionally trained professionals often overlook this aspect of medical treatment of mental health concerns. Currently, several Food and Drug Administration (FDA) approved genetic tests are available to assist in determining whether an individual's genetic make-up matches with a particular class of medications. More often than not, those who don't respond to medication are not taking the correct form. Like anything else, specific training is necessary for practitioners to become skilled in interpreting and applying the results of these genetic tests. I'm often the one who suggests to clients that they seek a professional who is skilled in using these tools, especially when their symptoms don't seem well managed despite other physical efforts.

Also, a high correlation of gastrointestinal issues exists for those who suffer from anxiety. While irritable bowel syndrome (IBS) isn't necessarily caused by anxiety, the link is well established and should be considered as an additional aspect of overall treatment of anxiety when both are present. Stress and anxiety activate the central nervous system, which in turn, releases hormones that can affect digestive processes in your gut. This can cause diarrhea, constipation, gas and discomfort. When the gut "biome" or environment is disrupted, it can cause not only GI upset but also cause a person to become anxious about leaving their home, hosting events, etc. for fear of having an uncontrollable episode. "Gut health" also plays a major role in whether an individual is able to absorb medication through their intestinal walls. Some people are prescribed high doses of medications to manage symptoms, but the ability to absorb and utilize the medications is not considered. All of these aspects of treating the body should be assessed when exploring treatment for anxiety disorders.

Three other medications are emerging as treatment possibilities for anxiety:

Ketamine

First used for anesthesia during surgery, ketamine was later found to have a rapid-acting effect for anxiety. Considered a medical psychedelic medicine, this drug targets different subsets of neurotransmitters in the brain than SSRIs, so patients who haven't experienced positive results from traditional medications sometimes experience improvement of symptoms with treatment. Ketamine is most commonly delivered in one of two ways: as an intravenous (IV) infusion or through an intranasal spray. It is administered either alone or with a therapeutic practitioner present (usually a psychotherapist or psychiatrist). A third option includes a brief administration of Transcranial Magnetic Stimulation (TMS—to be discussed later in this chapter) soon after the Ketamine is administered. While positive results are possible, this medication is still undergoing research for long-term efficacy as well as longstanding side-effect profile. Ketamine treatment is usually recommended only for those who have not experienced notable relief from other methods.

Other Psychedelic Treatments

Psychedelic medicines—another subclass of hallucinogenic drugs—are also being studied as potential FDA approved methods of treatment for certain kinds of anxiety, while Post-Traumatic Stress Disorder (no longer considered an anxiety disorder) being the primary concern of interest. These drugs produce changes in perception, mood and cognitive processes. Again, although promising results have been found, close monitoring and more research is required to learn more about the possibilities for treatment of anxiety. Many types of psychedelic medicines are currently under review (LSD, DMT, psilocybin or magic mushrooms, mescaline, 2C-B, 2C-1, 5 MeO-DMT, AMT, ibogaine and DOM). As of the writing of this book, the body of high-quality evidence on psychedelic therapy remains relatively small.

Note: It should be noted that psychedelics have been used for many years as a way to induce what many would consider to be a spiritual experience. First used by ancient cultures, these populations valued the ability to seemingly connect with the spiritual realm at a very deep level. Modern use of psychedelics has become a trend, as more people desire to experience something close to spiritual enlightenment. Although many claim to reach heightened levels of consciousness, it should be noted that psychedelic substances are hallucinogenic in nature. Research indicates that the expectation a person has when using the substance is strongly related to the outcome of the experience. For example, if a person expects to have a positive or spiritual outcome, they generally perceive that they do; the same is true if an individual expects a scary or negative reaction—their experience may terrify them. Therefore, it is important to consider whether a perceived spiritual experience under the influence of a psychedelic medicine is pure or simply drug-induced.

It is also important to consider how those with mental health conditions can be negatively—and sometime permanently impacted by the use of psychedelic substances. Speaking as a professional, a client chose to try a psychedelic medicine on her own without supervision, professional advice, nor awareness of how the substance could potentially harm her. Unfortunately, it was not a good outcome. She was hospitalized for both suicidal and homicidal ideation and never returned to her previous level of function thereafter. Her anxiety turned to far worse things and all aspects of her life were negatively and permanently impacted. If you are interested in knowing more about psychedelic treatment of anxiety, talk to your medical professional or specialist who can assess whether this approach is right for you.

CANNABIDIOL (CBD)

CBD is considered a pharmacologically broad-spectrum drug that has drawn increasing interest in recent years in the treatment of many neuropsychiatric disorders. Preclinical evidence supports the use of CBD in the treatment of Generalized Anxiety Disorder (GAD), panic disorder and social anxiety disorders, but research is limited. Many individuals likely self-manage anxiety using this substance, but more clinical studies need to be done to effectively establish the pros and cons of using CBD to treat anxiety.

Transcranial Magnetic Stimulation (TMS)

TMS is a fairly new, non-invasive treatment option for those who experience co-occurring anxiety and depressive symptoms and is used when other less intensive treatments have not helped. The method includes daily twenty-minute sessions for several weeks, using an electromagnetic coil close to the skull to deliver magnetic pulses into the brain. The pulses alter nerve cell activity in areas of the brain that are involved in mood regulation. While TMS has been extensively studied for the treatment of resistant forms of depression, fewer studies have been done related to anxiety. However, a recent systematic review of already completed studies does support TMS for treating generalized anxiety and the situation-induced manifestation of post-traumatic stress. Several of my clients have undergone this treatment with very positive results in managing their symptoms. None have reported complete resolution.

Possible Negative Impact of Body-Based Treatment

While there is certainly a need to manage severe symptoms of anxiety, often clients report so much dampening of emotion that they cannot emote even in situationally-appropriate circumstances. Symptom relief is necessary to experience quality of life, but in some cases the medications go too far in masking deeper origins of concerns. For instance, as mentioned before, everything is energy and if unresolved emotions are left unattended or expressed, it could damage the essence of an individual even more, hamper their healing or block their evolution beyond their concerns. Certain treatments also leave a person feeling dull, even when joyous occasions should make them feel otherwise. It is a fine balance to manage the body-based treatments of anxiety-related conditions, while identifying whether the soul needs to heal as well. We need skilled practitioners to help identify the difference. Increased understanding of all aspects of healing—body, mind and soul—will assist both those who struggle with anxiety and those who treat them to create a path to whole person health.

Natural Health, The Body and Anxiety

Many holistic health practitioners and researchers have studied how nutrition affects mental health. Much research indicates that inflammation in the body significantly contributes to the experience of anxiety. Further, many studies have shown that various vitamin deficiencies are correlated with anxiety, depression and other mental health concerns. In this case, it is important to consider how both food is medicine and how "junk in" may, in fact, create an experience of "junk out" (i.e., a negative response when not maintaining a healthy diet). Over the last ten years, the vast majority of my continuing education training for ongoing psychological licensure has surrounded the field of nutrition and mental health, including a specialized certification I received in Mental Health Nutrition. "Whole soul" health includes the body, and all components are important in treating anxiety, the most commonly diagnosed concern in America. Below are more things to consider when addressing anxiety.

Caffeine

Much research has been done related to the effect of caffeine on mood and cognitive function. Studies have long shown a direct connection with use and an increase in anxious symptoms for most anxiety disorders. Anyone who has a diagnosis of anxiety should consider reducing and/or eliminating it from their diet. Even small amounts of caffeine and other stimulants can have a negative impact on those who experience anxiety.

Inflammation in the body

Inflammation is part of the body's natural defense mechanism that is triggered when the immune system recognizes and removes harmful and foreign stimuli. Inflammation can be chronic or acute and has been linked to changes in the brain, including neurotransmitter function that affects mood, emotional reactions and memory. Although more research is necessary, scientists have found direct links between inflammation and anxiety.

Inflammation related to anxiety is generally caused by an overabundance in harmful or foreign toxins and is linked with excessive consumption of sugar products, artificial substances and/or processed foods. Both nutritional changes and routine exercise have been shown to significantly reduce inflammation, thus improving the symptoms of anxiety.

The anti-inflammatory diet has received much attention in the last few decades as a result of understanding the link between many medical and mental health conditions. Several anti-inflammatory foods are suggested to offer additional support to reduce the symptoms of anxiety: fatty fish like salmon, nuts like almonds and walnuts, leafy greens like spinach and kale and fruits like blueberries, strawberries and pomegranates.

My "go to" expert for information regarding inflammation and mental health is Dr. Andrew Weil, founder of the Andrew Weil Center for Integrative Medicine, located in Tucson, Arizona. For decades, he has led the way in understanding how natural approaches to the treatment of both medical and mental health disorders is essential to overall health. I've read several of his books, attended conferences in which he spoke and watched endless videos he offers on the subject of integrative health. He provides a down-to-earth application of complex approaches to health, making integration of his ideas very easy.

Vitamin Deficiency

Many vitamin deficiencies have been linked to anxiety, particularly for those living in the United States. Many experts now educate the public regarding the connection between mood and food. Below are the most commonly noted deficiencies related to anxiety-based concerns.

> **Magnesium** – Magnesium has been shown to be the number one vitamin deficiency related to anxiety for many potential reasons. This vitamin helps to control the chemical messengers (neurotransmitters) in the brain, resulting in a naturally occurring calming effect on the body. Magnesium also

helps manage stress responses and cortisol levels, so those with low levels of magnesium in their body may experience higher levels of both physical and mental stress. This vitamin is an essential nutrient for muscle function and the ability of muscles to relax. It also has regulating properties for the neurotransmitter GABA that is important for sleep.

People with anxiety may benefit by taking magnesium supplements and/or increasing certain foods in their diet (leafy greens such as spinach and Swiss chard, legumes, nuts and nut products, seeds and whole grains, artichokes, avocado, bananas, chicken breast, potatoes, raisins, tofu and yogurt).

Zinc—Eating foods rich in zinc have also been linked to lower levels of anxiety. Zinc is a mineral that has been shown to have protective effects against oxidative stress, which has links to anxiety and individuals with deficiency, tend to have higher levels of anxiety. Foods rich in zinc include oysters, cashews, liver, beef and egg yolks.

Omega-3—Omega-3 fatty acids have been shown to decrease inflammation in the body as mentioned earlier. While researchers knew it helped with depression, it wasn't until a study was done with medical students in 2011 that Omega-3s were first found to help with anxiety as well. Many foods are beneficial: fatty fish (such as salmon, mackerel, tuna, herring and sardines), nuts and seeds (such as flaxseed, chia seeds and walnuts) and plant oils (such as flaxseed oil, soybean oil and canola oil).

B Vitamins—Three of the B vitamins have been linked to anti-anxiety effects: B6, B9 and B12. While all of the B vitamins are necessary for different aspects of health, only these three have been directly linked to decreasing anxiety. B6 has been shown to assist in serotonin production, B9, also known as folic acid, and B12 have both been linked to anxiety when deficiency is present.

Foods rich in the respective vitamins are listed. B6: beef liver, tuna, salmon, chickpeas, poultry, dark leafy greens, bananas, papayas, oranges and cantaloupes. B9: dark green leafy vegetables (turnip greens, spinach, romaine lettuce, brussel sprouts, broccoli) beans, peanuts, and sunflower seeds. B12 include: fish, meat, poultry, eggs and dairy products.

Probiotic Foods—Research has also shown that eating probiotic-rich foods can also help
in lowering anxiety. Gut health has been the focus of holistic research for years and has been linked to both anxiety and depression. Those with leaky gut syndrome or chronic bowel issues tend to have an unbalanced or upset biome in their stomach and intestinal tract. Often probiotic supplements or probiotic-rich foods can help to restore a healthy balance, thus decreasing anxiety symptoms. Foods such as onions, garlic, apples, under ripe bananas, oatmeal, asparagus, yogurt, kefir, sauerkraut, tempeh, buttermilk, pickles and more can be helpful to consume.

While food alone won't cure anxiety, there is good evidence that it is a piece of the puzzle when managing anxiety.

Natural Supplements

For centuries, natural supplements created in the form of tea and tinctures have been used to treat various mental and physical concerns. With anxiety in mind, many of these supplements are still effective today, but are more commonly recommended to be taken in capsule or tablet form for consistency and regulation. Natural supplements are not habit-forming which means in many ways, they can be safer than some medications. However, because the chemistry of many herbal remedies is complex, the mechanisms of action (what makes them work) are not always known. However, there are no toxic or adverse effects for most supplements.

Some medical professionals are open to the use of herbal supplements as an adjunct attempt to treat anxiety, but most practitioners are not formally educated about holistic methods. Consultation with an herbalist, holistic medical provider, naturopath or other naturally-based professional may be helpful in determining whether a natural supplement is right for you. It is important to also seek guidance for whether natural supplements interact with prescribed medications. Pharmacists can be extremely beneficial in helping you determine whether there is a concern.

> **Valerian**-Valerian root (Valeriana officinalis) is derived from the root of a European plant and has been used for centuries to promote a sense of calm, relaxation and sleep. This remedy has been shown to be effective in treating anxiety and can be safely used with antidepressants.
>
> **Kava**-Like Valerian, Kava (Piper methysticum) is another root supplement that offers sedative or calming effects. It is derived from a tropical plant that is related to black pepper and has also been used for many years as an anti-anxiety

remedy. In randomized control trials with humans, it has been shown to be as effective as benzodiazepine drugs in the treatment of anxiety. One concern for using kava relates to rare cases of liver toxicity, so those with a history of liver disease are discouraged from using this supplement.

Ashwagandha- This supplement is often called Indian Ginseng and its use is widely known in what is called Ayurvedic medicine, a centuries-old traditional system of providing medical care in India. The Ayurvedic approach promotes the attention of diet and lifestyle as main managers of health concerns. Ashwagandha (Withania somnifera) is widely known for its tonic and stress-protective support and is often used for its "sleep bearing" (somnifera) calming action. Ashwagandha can also be safely used with antidepressants, but there is some concern when autoimmune issues are present.

Holy Basil-This herb, also known as tulsi (Ocimum sanctum) is a sacred plant from India that is planted near Hindu temples and around homes in honor of the deity Vishnu. It has anti-inflammatory effects and protects the body and brain from negative aspects of stress. Much like others, this herb can be safely used with antidepressants.

5-HTP-5-hydroxytryptophan (5-HTP) is a byproduct of the protein building block L-tryptophan, which tends to have calming properties. It comes from the seeds of an African plant (Griffonia simplicifolia) and works in the brain and nervous system by increasing the production of serotonin. Many holistic practitioners endorse the use of 5-HTP to treat both anxiety and depression.

L-Theanine-L-Theanine is an amino acid found in black and green teas that has been shown to support stressful responses and promote relaxation. Holistic practitioners endorse the supplement as an agent that quickly reduces mental stress and helps to settle the mind. While research supports the use of this supplement, it is less known. L-Theanine is often found in melatonin supplements for sleep.

Passion Flower- Passiflora incarnata (Passion Flower) is a perennial plant that has been shown to have therapeutic properties when taken as a supplement. Research indicates that is has significant positive effects when treating anxiety. Due to its calming properties, this supplement has been used to treat general stress, anxiety, depression and insomnia.

Lemon Balm- Lemon balm (Melissa officinalis) is a member of the mint family and is considered a calming herb. As early as the Middle Ages, it was used to reduce stress and anxiety and promote sleep. Current research indicates great benefit when used to reduce clinically-diagnosed anxiety.

Like medication, supplements have been found to reduce the symptoms of anxiety in many individuals, but not completely eliminate the negative experience. More research is necessary; however, when considering the complexity of anxiety, it makes sense to explore all options. I always encourage clients to discuss options with credentialed professionals when seeking advice, but keep in mind that drug interactions may present an issue. I've simply listed the most commonly used supplements for educational purposes, not as encouragement to take them without professional advice.

Yoga and other Movement Therapies

Many individuals who struggle with anxiety engage in various movement therapies to reduce their symptoms. Yoga, Tai Chi, Qigong and other forms have all undergone research to determine the effectiveness of using such methods. While studies indicate positive outcomes, the research is limited due to loose methodology, low numbers of participants and inability to filter other factors that might account for firm determination of efficacy. Regardless, these modalities should be included for anyone interested, given their multifactorial benefit including social support, time to get the mind off of anxiety-provoking situations and general self-care.

Massage/Therapeutic Touch

Few would say massage doesn't work to reduce stress and anxiety. Research agrees. Although therapeutic touch is one of the most sought-out forms of complementary approaches, the effectiveness in reducing anxiety hadn't been researched until 2010. Studies now show a direct and significant reduction in anxiety symptoms, particularly for generalized anxiety disorder (GAD). While massage alone doesn't eliminate anxiety, significant reduction of anxious symptoms is clearly evident.

Acupuncture

The practice of traditional Chinese medicine (TCM) is centuries old. It is based on treating the individual's conditions in relation to particular patterns of displayed symptoms. In addition to a "pulse" diagnosis, the identification of particular energetic points on an individual's body that may indicate imbalance or blockage is key. Acupuncture, or the gentle placement of acupuncture needles, is designed to either unblock energy points or help energy move more easily between them. Recent systematic reviews of studies, including meta-analysis, show very positive results for reduction of anxiety symptoms. Because many Chinese medicine professionals practice acupuncture and provide consultation regarding herbal supplements, it is possible to greatly reduce anxiety symptoms when visiting these practitioners.

It is not possible to describe every possible method of reducing anxiety that is related to treating the body. As you can already see, there are many ways to address symptoms that arise and persist, but finding the cause may require other action. While emotional relief is important in managing the symptoms of anxiety, it is important to recognize that people often use medication to dampen the voice of their soul—the part that is trying to alert them of the discomfort or damage experienced deep within.

Messages from the Body

Sometimes individuals who suffer from emotional concerns don't want to experience what disrupts them, but these reactions actually provide the information necessary to heal. The voice of the soul often carries the information about what first created their concerns, which offers the information necessary to help an individual heal at the deepest level. On the other hand, for some, it takes medication to calm the body and mind enough to listen more deeply. Because every individual is different, understanding the interplay between the body, mind and soul aspects of healing is essential to help a person restore to whole health. Also, understanding the critical balance of each is often essential in creating whole soul health.

Considering soul healing as an additional aspect of care for anxiety disorders has the potential to possibly minimize or even eliminate the need for ongoing traditional care. Finding a way to explore the origin of anxiety takes finesse and skill beyond what traditional medical treatment can offer. This is where soul-healing techniques might be necessary to fully excavate and understand an individual's wounds. As traditional and soul-healing professionals learn to work together, much more progress will be made in treating anxiety and other mental health concerns.

The next chapter explores treating the mind as an additional aspect of whole person treatment of anxiety.

CHAPTER FIVE

TREATING THE MIND AND MODERN ANXIETY

It's ruinous for the soul to be anxious about the future...
For such a soul will never be at rest.

SENECA

You can't just tell someone to stop feeling anxious. They need to identify and address what causes their unrest. For years, traditionally trained practitioners have struggled to help clients find what triggers their reactions and while huge strides have been made to develop various forms of psychological treatment, often even those fall short in eliminating discomfort. While treatment of the body and mind have helped many people manage their symptoms, very few feel they are completely cured.

Mind-Based Approaches for Treating Anxiety

Several types of psychotherapeutic treatment exist to address anxiety-related concerns. These are described here, along with many other adjunctive approaches that have been shown to reduce symptoms. All mind-based approaches focus on retraining the brain to respond differently to both anxiety-provoking stimuli and to physical and mental symptoms that arise. As a mental health professional, I have been trained in most of the theories and techniques listed below. Still, some clients need strategies that reach deeper to further relieve their symptoms. Much more will be discussed about soul-based options later. First, following is a review of the most used psychotherapeutic options.

Cognitive-Behavioral Therapy

Cognitive-Behavioral Therapy (CBT) is the most commonly used form of therapy and much research has been done to explore the benefit of helping individuals change how they think so they can behave differently as a result. Aaron T. Beck developed cognitive therapy in the 1960's to treat depression and it has since been adapted to assist with anxious symptoms as well. Although a genetic predisposition to anxiety might exist, CBT holds the tenet that changing perceptions about how to see and manage our thoughts about life will improve our experience of anxious symptoms. Because how we think about life affects life satisfaction, CBT aims to "correct" and reframe thought patterns in a more positive direction. Distorted thinking, the tendency to exaggerate or "awfulize" our experiences is a primary focus of cognitive therapy in the treatment of anxiety. Various techniques have been developed to assist patients in minimizing these thought patterns.

Many relaxation and calming strategies are integrated into CBT, along with many thought-stopping techniques. Some include stress reduction techniques, self-monitoring, activity scheduling (to plan for and avoid stressful reactions to certain events), documenting thought patterns, role-playing to practice emotional regulation, cognitive reframing/reshaping (to shift from negative thoughts to positive ones), identification of trigger thoughts and events, identifying unhealthy core beliefs, recognition of cognitive distortions, identifying cognitive distortions and more.

Specific offshoot forms of CBT have been developed over the years and some will be discussed below.

Relaxation Response

Herbert Benson, a cardiologist and founder of Harvard University's Mind/Body Medical Institute, identified that it is possible to reduce stress and anxiety by increasing blood flow to the brain. His studies in the 1960's and 1970's focused on this phenomenon, which he called the "Relaxation Response", and led to his development of The Stress Reduction and Relaxation Response protocol. This mind/body approach mixed deep-breathing techniques with strategies to change thoughts related to the fight-or-flight response to stress. The response is defined as a creating a personal ability to encourage the body to release chemicals and brain signals to make a person's muscles and organs slow down to increase blood flow to the brain. Mixing CBT techniques with this particular strategy has been shown to be effective in treating a wide range of stress and anxiety-related disorders.

Through his work, Benson is largely credited for demystifying meditation and helping to bring it into the mainstream treatment of various concerns. Along with improvement in general stress and anxiety, his work showed that the Relaxation Response increased overall wellbeing and also reduced blood pressure and resting heart rate for anyone struggling with stress.

I first heard Dr. Benson speak while completing a post-doctoral fellowship in Family Medicine at the University of Missouri. Two years later, after accepting a job as the Director of Behavioral Science in Family Medicine at Wake Forest University School of Medicine, I received specialized training at the Mind-Body Medical Institute at Harvard University with Dr. Benson. To this day, I use many of the strategies I learned while receiving my certification. As I developed my own strategies to do deeper soul-healing work with clients, I integrated some of the centering techniques I learned in 2002. To me, this is proof that treating body, mind and soul can be accomplished while blending medical, psychological and soul-healing techniques.

Mindfulness-Based Cognitive Therapy (MBCT)

Jon Kabat-Zinn, a molecular biologist, first developed Mindfulness-Based Stress Reduction (MBSR) after learning meditation around 1979. He founded the Stress Reduction Clinic at the University of Massachusetts Medical School where he developed structured programs and research related to the positive impact of meditation on many physical and emotional concerns. He emphasized that mindfulness techniques, strategies designed to increase awareness and consciousness about something, can decrease emotional discomfort. Mindfulness-Based Cognitive Therapy (MBCT) was created to use mindfulness strategies to reduce symptoms of many mental health concerns and has been shown to significantly decrease the negative experience of anxiety-related disorders.

I also received training in both MBSR and MBCT and have utilized many of the strategies for various psychological concerns. Kabat-Zinn's book, Full Catastrophe Living, describes his strategies for MBCT and explains how mindfulness and meditation can be effective in treating various health and mental health disorders.

Dialectical Behavioral Therapy (DBT)

DBT is another specific form of Cognitive Behavioral Therapy. Marsha Linehan, an American psychologist, blended cognitive restructuring with acceptance, mindfulness and reshaping of thoughts. It was originally developed to treat borderline personality disorder, a highly emotionally reactive concern, but because one of the main goals is to help a person change behavior patterns, it is now sometimes used to treat those who experience anxiety. Linehan was diagnosed with schizophrenia early in adulthood, which led to her interest in seeking an education to help others. Through the early part of her career, she self-determined that her symptoms at the time of hospitalization more closely described borderline personality disorder and not schizophrenia. She aimed to develop a treatment strategy that could minimize or eliminate the necessity to use medication as part of healing, hence the birth of her DBT approach. Her work led to educating the public about Dialectical Behavioral Therapy in the 1970's with wider acceptance since around 2015.

DBT is particularly helpful for people with anxiety disorders who struggle with self-harm and other seriously negative coping habits. Mindfulness techniques are part of treatment since these strategies can assist in regulating emotional responses.

Acceptance and Commitment Therapy (ACT)

ACT is a relatively new form of Cognitive Behavioral Therapy designed by American psychologist, Steven Hayes around 1982. The approach was initially called comprehensive distancing and included a mixture of cognitive strategies with behavioral analysis. ACT includes various protocols depending on the behavior that is being targeted for change and is not based on the elimination of discomfort; rather, it focuses on ways to remain present with what life brings. In this way, it resembles mindfulness-based strategies. The added layer is that ACT aims to instill acceptance of the uncomfortable experiences and teaches ways to prevent overreaction to undesirable responses or avoidance of them. The core intention of this form of treatment is to create greater appreciation and understanding of emotions, while helping an individual create meaning of the emotions experienced as part of moving forward in life. "Values-guided action" and "mindful action" are terms used in ACT. This form of treatment teaches six core therapeutic concepts: contacting the present moment, defusion (separating ourselves from our thoughts), acceptance of the negative experience, self as concept (being able to observe oneself), value of what really matters with regard to reactions and behavior change, and the process of values-congruent action (basing reactions of an individual's value system). Popularity of ACT is increasing as more practitioners become trained in using this approach with their clients.

Exposure Therapy

Exposure therapy is a form of behavioral therapy used to assist those who struggle with anxiety disorders and phobias and involves encouraging an individual to face what they fear, either imagined or in real life, while under the guidance of a trained professional in a safe environment. This approach exposes individuals to their fears in increments based on discussion with the person about what would be minimally to extremely disturbing. The therapist helps the individual explore anxiety-provoking thoughts while being guided to use various stress-reducing techniques in the presence of the uncomfortable stimuli or object of fear. For instance, if a person fears dogs, a therapist would assist a patient in creating ranked levels of exposure to systematically work on decreasing anxiety responses with each level. This might include first looking at a picture of a dog then working up to direct interaction with one or more.

Exposure Therapy is based on research by Russian scientist, Ivan Pavlov in the early 1900's who discovered that animals can be either programmed to respond with fear or desensitized from fearful responses. His work explained what he called "classical conditioning", and has served as the basis for many behavioral treatments since that time. While modern exposure therapy now incorporates cognitive strategies as well, this system of treatment is effective in the treatment of phobias, panic disorder, social anxiety disorder and generalized anxiety disorder (GAD). It has also shown positive response for post-traumatic stress disorder (PTSD), which is now categorized as a trauma- and stressor-related disorder, and obsessive-compulsive disorder (OCD), an obsessive-compulsive and related disorder.

Rational Emotive Behavior Therapy (REBT)

American psychologist Albert Ellis developed what was originally called Rational Emotive Therapy in the mid-1950s, following his work to reduce or eliminate negative or unhealthy thought patterns. REBT focuses on managing irrational thoughts, emotions and behaviors and contrasts from passive approaches that emphasize thoughts alone. REBT is an active process designed to identify and eliminate unhelpful thought patterns and behaviors linked to self-defeating thoughts and feelings. Ellis developed short-term strategies aimed to eliminate challenging thought patterns within five sessions when possible. REBT aims to improve problem-solving skills, restructure problematic thoughts and increase overall coping skills.

Rational Emotive Behavior Therapy is shown to be effective in various anxiety-related concerns in which faulty thinking is the core of the issue.

Interpersonal Therapy

Interpersonal Therapy (IPT) was first developed in the 1970's by psychiatrist Gerald Klerman, researcher Myrna Weissman and their colleagues. It was initially designed as a treatment for major depression in adults, but it has also been shown to be effective in treating certain kinds of anxiety disorders, particularly social anxiety disorder.

The core principle of IPT is that relationships and life events directly impact mood, which effect interactions. IPT focuses on current relationships with important contacts and aims to improve the quality of a person's interpersonal relationships by reducing overall distress. Strategies include structured, short-term therapy designed to improve perceptions of how interactions will go, practical management of symptoms and increasing a sense of control in interpersonal situations.

Emotional Freedom Technique (EFT)

EFT has become increasingly popular since the 1990's. Sometimes called tapping, Emotional Freedom Technique combines traditional cognitive strategies with stimulation of acupressure points by pressuring, tapping or rubbing them while focusing on images that represent personal fear or trauma. The technique draws from several treatment methods including exposure therapy and various theories of alternative medicine treatments—including acupuncture (use of needles to stimulate pressure points), energy medicine (strategies to unblock a person's energy centers in the body) and Thought Field Therapy (described below). Holistic Practitioner, Gary Craig first developed the strategy and various mental health practitioners have embraced the positive results found for many emotional concerns.

The technique usually entails five steps: 1) identifying the issue, 2) evaluating the intensity in which it is experienced, 3) creating a mantra to repeat when experiencing disturbance, 4) learning a tapping sequence (based on already-identified acupressure points) and 5) evaluating the intensity at which the concern is experienced after the tapping procedure has been completed.

While a trained practitioner provides initial treatment, EFT can be used at any time once the strategies have been learned. While more research is necessary, some studies have shown significant reduction in anxiety symptoms particularly for specific stress-inducing stimuli.

Eye Movement Desensitization and Reprocessing (EMDR)

EMDR has received much attention since it's development in 1987 by Francine Shapiro. The strategy was created to treat trauma-based disorders such as post-traumatic stress. Research has shown improvement in anxiety symptoms for other disorders as well.

EMDR is a short-term, experiential therapy that targets reducing distressing experiences and memories by changing the emotional intensity in which the brain experiences the stressor. Unlike traditional psychotherapy, clients don't delve deeply into painful experiences; instead, they undergo bilateral stimulation of the brain through specific eye moments or tapping experiences. Therapists may incorporate mindfulness strategies, along with meditation or other relaxation techniques. Cognitive-behavioral therapy often complements EMDR by restructuring unhealthy thought patterns. Those with anxiety generally feel a heightened sense of control, a decrease in emotional and physical tension and less intrusive stressful or traumatic memories.

EMDR is shown to be effective in treating generalized anxiety (GAD) to decrease persistent and excessive worry, panic disorder to decrease frequency and severity of symptoms and phobias to address tension related to imagined concerns. In all cases, treatment focuses on positively altering the brain's information processing system associated with negative thoughts, emotions and body sensations, thereby reducing overall experience of symptoms.

Summary of Mind-Based Approaches to Treating Anxiety

Much like some of the body-based treatment strategies, some of the methods mentioned above could, in fact, block full healing when it comes to a soul-based origin of anxiety disorders. While changing negative or traumatic thoughts is part of the healing process, the elimination of emotions might dampen the ability to use them to identify deeper origins of anxiety. This could be why some anxiety-related conditions persist even after years of treatment. In a later chapter, I explain how an "energetic imprint" can be left on the soul by an acutely stressful or traumatic event. When unattended, this imprint can cause persistence of discomfort or relapse of symptoms later in life, particularly if/when another stressful event occurs.

Regardless, mind-based strategies are necessary to assist in treating anxiety-related disorders. Talking about the different aspects of healing is sometimes helpful in itself. However, the integration of soul-based methods might be the key in eliminating the concern, not just treating symptoms.

Complementary Treatment of Anxiety

As mentioned, many complementary treatments have been integrated into formal treatment of anxiety disorders, including meditation, relaxation, energy strategies, acupuncture and acupressure. A few of these are highlighted as adjunct treatment strategies.

Meditation

Throughout history, many cultures have used meditation as part of daily practice, problem solving and resolution of discomfort. Meditation involves focusing the attention on a single word, object, sensation, sound, etc. then letting go of the distracting thoughts and feelings that interfere with attention. Buddhist meditation promotes the importance of this exercise to stop thoughts and free the mind of stressful images and experiences. Other forms of meditation aim to do different things to decrease suffering. Many advanced individuals claim to reach the highest states of consciousness as a result of strict practice. While western cultures do not usually practice meditation, these strategies have shown great success in quieting the brain, reducing physical symptoms related to stress and anxiety and improving overall life satisfaction. Many forms of meditation exist, including walking and running meditation for those who wish to incorporate these strategies into more active forms of stress or anxiety reduction.

Many online options now exist to guide meditations. I suggest these often for people who want to quiet their minds for even as little as five minutes a day.

Author Eckhart Tolle said, "The stream of thinking has enormous momentum that can easily drag you along with it." Meditation strategies can assist anyone who struggles with anxiety to slow thoughts to a much more manageable and controllable pace.

Relaxation Strategies

Relaxation strategies are therapeutic strategies designed to reduce tension and anxiety. Many practitioners incorporate relaxation into their work to help the individual feel a greater sense of calm. Following are a few to consider:

Breathwork—Trained breathing includes various methods of taking in slow, deep or rhythmic breaths to calm the nervous system.

Progressive Muscle Relaxation (PMR)—PMR is the systematic tensing and relaxing of different muscle groups, starting from the feet to face or vice versa. It induces a relaxed state both physically and mentally.

Yoga—Mentioned in the previous chapter, many yoga instructors include relaxation strategies depending on the form of yoga being taught. While a series of physical poses are completed to enhance flexibility, strength and balance, breathing exercises and meditation techniques are often also incorporated.

Music Therapy—Music and vibrational therapy includes listening to or using instruments to soothe, uplift or inspire an individual. Music can also be used to release and express emotions (drumming, rattles, or any instrument).

Visualization/Guided imagery—These strategies involve imagining a peaceful and pleasant scene, such as a beach, a forest, or a mountain, and using all the senses to experience it. Visualization can be practiced alone, but many wonderful pre-recorded journeys are available online or in groups.

Tai chi/Qigong—Integrative mental health practitioners sometimes teach these forms of movement as part of anxiety-reduction training. These movement therapies involve either performing a series of slow and graceful movements that flow from one to another, while breathing deeply and focusing on the present moment or by making more active movements paired with breathwork to release stress from a particular part of the body. Both are very effective in reducing stress and anxiety.

Mantram—This strategy refers to the practice of silently or quietly repeating certain syllables or phrases in a way to distract the mind from intrusive or stressful thoughts. Chanting, most often associated with eastern traditions focuses on releasing the "monkey mind" and entering into a state of enlightenment. Regardless of whether one reaches such a state, mantras can be incredibly helpful in redirecting unhealthy thoughts and decreasing both stress and anxiety.

Reiki/Energy Work—Reiki is a Japanese strategy developed specifically for stress reduction and relaxation. It is based on assisting an individual in moving blocked or sluggish "life force energy" that flows through us. Some integrative mental health practitioners use Reiki or other forms of energy work to help clients work through various mental health concerns, anxiety being one of the main complaints. It is administered by laying hands on an individual to sense and access the energy centers throughout the body that correlate to emotional concerns. Numerous forms of energy therapy are now widely accepted as adjunctive treatment for anxiety and other mental health concerns.

As you can see, many forms of psychotherapeutic strategies exist to manage symptoms of anxiety. None have been shown to cure the condition.

Messages from the Mind

As mentioned previously, although many of the modalities described above are designed to minimize emotional reaction, sometimes the key to what first caused the reaction lies in the emotion itself. The soul often speaks through our human emotions and thoughts to alert us to deep wounds and often a person must access and acknowledge them to identify what is really at the core of a reaction. The most ideal approach to treating anxiety from a mind perspective is to consider that all aspects of whole health—body mind and soul—might be playing a part in an individual's experience of anxiety.

Soul-healing methods often assist an individual in identifying the core of their concerns. This will be discussed more in the next two sections. The next chapter explores *The Three Levels of Healing* that are necessary for full resolution of concerns.

CHAPTER SIX

THE THREE LEVELS OF HEALING AND THE TAPESTRY OF LIFE

The human mind has a desire to know its place in the universe and the role we play in the tapestry of life.
MICHIO KAKU

Theoretical physicist, Michio Kaku doesn't study the soul, but he does try to answer some of the biggest questions posed by humans. He understands that we want answers and that many of them are woven deeply into the complexity of overall life.

When individual fields of study try to solve dilemmas, they only see possible solutions from their area of focus or expertise. The scientific method—the systematic observation, measurement and experiment and the formulation, testing and modification of hypotheses—typically tightens the lens on one particular aspect of an issue. This may provide small pieces of the puzzle, but the entire picture remains out of view. When multiple aspects of a problem exist, such as the complexity of anxiety and other mental health disorders, the search for understanding can obscure what is present beyond a microscopic interpretation. In this case, it is the soul that has been overlooked. It is time for traditional, holistic and spiritually oriented practitioners to join forces to weave a more comprehensive approach to solving the question of how to more fully treat anxiety and other mental health concerns.

Before exploring the tapestry of mental health more fully, it is important to explain the levels of healing that are necessary for full resolution of concerns.

The Three Levels of Healing

The week prior to writing this chapter I had a fourth session with a new client, a physician who sought my services to discuss how to rebalance her life following the pandemic. She came upon my website, which highlights my most recent book, *The Healer's Path to Post Recovery: A Restorative Journey for Healthcare Providers*. Because of both this and the fact that I include spiritual exploration as part of my practice, she felt I'd be a good fit to help her rebuild. In the midst of getting to know her, she mentioned some traumatic events she experienced in the past. She said she couldn't understand why after all this time, including a few years in therapy, she still had intense responses to certain situations that reminded her of that time. I shared with her my ideas about *The Three Levels of Healing* that I believe must be addressed in order for full recovery to occur. After hearing my explanation, she became tearful as she said it was the first thing that made sense to her in understanding the residual emotion she experiences. Even after all of the medical training she had, she'd never known that healing her soul was the key in releasing her from the ongoing emotional pain. Below is an explanation of *The Three Levels of Healing* that must be experienced to return to whole person health.

The First Level of Healing: Intellectual Healing

As Kaku stated, we all want to know our place in the universe. In the case of anxiety and all other mental health concerns, we what to know how and why it began. We can't really begin to heal unless we can connect the dots to understand: 1) what happened to initiate a problem, 2) what triggers it, 3) how to manage it, and 4) whether it will ever go away. These are also the typical steps taken when undergoing Cognitive Behavioral Therapy (CBT). With anxiety in mind, we usually scour our memory to determine the origin, look for and avoid similar situations, find ways to minimize the impact and hope it will never return. If we can't grasp how our process goes, we won't get better. It just won't happen. However, when we figure out why something has gone wrong, we can find a solution to either fix the problem or prevent it from happening again.

Simply put, *intellectual awareness* is mandatory for us to heal. It is the first step in re-establishing whole health. However, often this isn't enough to fully resolve our challenges. The First Level of Healing, then, is Intellectual Healing.

The Second Level of Healing: Emotional Healing

Once we have a basic understanding of how and why we experience what we do, we have to go about releasing the thoughts and emotions that come with our discomfort. In my book, *Soul Health: Aligning with Spirit for Radiant Living*, I talk about the importance of honoring emotions without pushing them away. The entire chapter about psychological health emphasizes the need to observe and understand what our emotions are trying to tell us in order to heal. Only when we extract the meaning behind a particular feeling and learn how to release those specific reactions do we find sustainable relief.

While CBT is helpful in changing faulty ways of thinking, it can often undercut the necessity of understanding that the emotion actually serves a greater purpose. Also, many medications are designed to alter the experience of emotion, sometimes to the point of preventing any or all expression. Many clients report feeling numb and unreactive, even when extremely challenging events arise. While this might be desirable in some cases, it isn't a natural expression of what a person should feel at the time. The fact is, emotion, when managed enough to observe and learn from it, informs us of what is truly misaligned or wounded deep inside.

Earlier in this book, you read about the importance of understanding energy as part of healing. Every emotion holds a certain charge, a different energetic frequency depending on which feeling is stirred. If unexpressed or unattended at the time we experience it, the energy of the emotion has to go somewhere—it gets stored in our body. This causes a "warehousing" effect, an energetic stockpiling deep within the essence of who we are. Sometimes we experience these residual emotions through the manifestation of physical concerns—stomach ulcers, heart palpitations, headaches, etc. and in other cases they are expressed through emotional conditions such as anxiety, post-traumatic stress and panic. Regardless of whether our stored emotions are reflected through emotional or physical concerns, they represent a misalignment of body, mind and soul. The very essence of who we are becomes flooded with our unresolved emotions, sometimes to the point that the dam breaks. If this happens, our soul can become fractured and wounded in such a way that we malfunction through either emotional or physical manifestation of conditions.

Therefore, the Second Level of Healing requires the action of *identifying and fully releasing or resolving emotions* that are stored within us, but in such a way that the meaning behind each is honored and understood. In other words, the energy of the emotion "stamps" our soul—the energetic essence of who we are—in such a way that it alters our ability to experience whole health.

For instance, when we have been betrayed, hurt or wounded, our emotions remain stored within us when left unsaid or unexpressed. Subsequent negative events can either trigger the original wound or add to the emotional pile. Much of both the psychological and soul-healing work I do includes the identification, honoring and removal of stored emotion while teaching clients how to interpret the meaning embedded in each. Sometimes the meaning stems from wounds or trauma in this lifetime, while in others it extends into past-life suffering, ancestral wounds and other soul-based injury. The soul can hold wounds from the current life or any prior lives, but all contribute to the manifestation and expression of mental health concerns in the present. It is the energy stored within that needs attention. This is why it is imperative for practitioners to understand the energy of the soul—the light within that dictates every thought, emotion and behavior. The more buried a person becomes under the wounds of their deepest self, the less brightly the soul shines and the more it misfires, which is often expressed in the experience of anxious symptoms. Only by exploring and releasing the emotion related to a specific wound does an individual find true relief. Sometimes there are many layers to remove before a person no longer experiences anxiety. As mentioned already, unfortunately some traditional protocols dampen emotions, making healing an unreachable outcome.

All of us are susceptible to carrying unresolved emotions because society isn't keen on expressing them or letting them go. As mentioned in earlier chapters, women in particular were required to keep their emotions to themselves. From an ancestral trauma perspective, many women still hold wounds that create fear in speaking their truth. Men have long been told not to cry or show any type of "weak" emotion. In different ways, both genders have suppressed their emotions to the point that each has manifested mental health issues or physical concerns.

These conditions may appear different depending on whether you are male or female, but it is clear that the internalization of emotions contributes greatly to how healthy a person feels.

The human condition—the totality of the experience of being human, including both good and bad involvements—is thickly laced with emotional events. Without constant maintenance, our emotions pile up. Identifying and releasing them is the only way to heal. It liberates us from anything that may mire or prevent our growth. Without level two of healing—*the identification and release of stored emotion*—it is impossible to feel better. You will not feel whole.

Therefore, The Second Level of Healing is Emotional Healing.

The Third Level of Healing: Soul Healing

Soul Healing, The Third Level of Healing, is the deepest level of healing possible; it is the most important in the full resolution of our concerns. As mentioned, sometimes our soul becomes fractured or wounded in such a way that it prevents us from feeling healthy no matter what we try or do—it blocks our ability to feel complete. Regardless of which traditional strategies we undergo, something continues to bog us down or trigger unwanted reactions. We continue to feel misaligned and vulnerable to experience further emotional turmoil. Our energetic framework is seemingly forever changed and feels doomed to misfire irrespective of other healing methods we attempt.

Because energy never goes away, it only changes, our wounds can turn into mounds of unresolvable pain that continue to interfere with everyday life. Unbeknownst to traditionally trained practitioners, soul wounds can fester, grow and create energetic blockages if left unattended. This results in unexplained physical and emotional concerns as well as the exacerbation of new wounds as they occur. Unfortunately, because relatively few practitioners attend to matters of the soul, most people go without the help they need to resolve their issues.

Understanding how soul injury can impact overall coping will be helpful as you read further. Our soul wounds inevitably affect how we experience the human condition. Take, for instance, the idea of a latent image—an "imprint" that is left from some anomaly, impact or event that might go unnoticed. While a person may appear to have healed from a physical injury from the outside, an X-Ray or magnetic resonance image (MRI) may show otherwise. Fingerprints aren't typically visible unless dusted and examined to study the details. Finally, the shadow left on paper by smudges on a copy machine might be hard to find and resolve unless you know where to look. In each case, you wouldn't try to find something you didn't know was there.

Soul wounds are much the same—you might not know to look more closely to identify the core cause of a concern without a hint that something deeper exists. Energetic "imprints" are left on the soul when deep wounding has occurred. The soul is "stamped" with the energy of trauma, betrayal or any other damaging event or interaction when left unresolved. Therefore, the energy of the wound remains until it is consciously removed as part of the healing process. The experience of anxiety, then, could be caused by an unseen disturbance when only examined from the traditional view. A wider lens complete with body, mind and soul in mind may be necessary to fully treat the condition.

In previous chapters, treatment of the body and mind were discussed in relation to anxiety and related disorders. While these treatments are shown to improve the symptoms associated with anxious reactions, they may not resolve the core of what created them in the first place. Because many body-based treatments focus on biochemically altering or quieting the symptoms of anxiety, they may mask what actually needs to be addressed from the soul level.

Much is the same for some psychological treatment approaches for anxiety; some methods aim to reduce or eliminate the emotional reaction to certain stimuli when, in fact, understanding that emotional reaction from a deeper perspective will lead you to what needs to be healed at the core.

In saying this, I am not suggesting that treatment methods that focus on the body and mind aspects of anxiety are not effective or necessary. I'm simply saying they may not be enough. In many cases, soul-based wounds prevent a deeper and more sustainable sense of resolution.

The Third Level of Healing—*Soul Healing*—will be discussed in detail throughout the remainder of this book. This is often the missing link in both medical and mental health concerns.

The Soul's Tapestry of Life

Our life is like a tapestry—it is woven according to what we experience from the beginning until the end. It holds the strings, colors and patterns that tell the story of our life, including the snags that indicate difficult times. Because each of us has lessons to learn—challenges that seem to be woven throughout our life—everyone's tapestry looks different. Our job as humans is to identify what disrupts the pattern of threads and learn to remove whatever gets in the way of maintaining the design that matches who we really are. In this way, the tapestry comes to represent how well we care for ourselves—how well we tend to our soul.

From a soul perspective, our tapestry begins not at the time we are born into a lifetime, but at the time in which our soul itself was created. The tapestry for this lifetime begins where the last left off and holds the lessons we must overcome in the current life. As we learn, heal and evolve, the tapestry changes. We study how to remove misaligned threads as we overcome challenges and master our life lessons, thus reweaving our fabric to represent a new way of life. If we are doing our work—overcoming challenges and healing both our human aspects and our soul—our textile will look much different by the end of life.

When left unattended, our tapestry fades, becomes a bit tattered and not much changes in the pattern. We continue to experience the same challenges over and over again because those troublesome threads have not been removed. If not healed, our soul becomes dull, as does our metaphorical tapestry of life.

While traditional therapies look at the tapestry only from where current life begins, soul-healing specialists explore the entirety of a woven pattern that may play a part in creating disruption now. They understand that today's discomfort often originates from past wounds or snags, with many factors playing a part in how a person's entire soul story has unfolded. The human condition is but one part of the tale.

Soul-healing practitioners also assist clients in identifying patterns that no longer serve them, helping the client to slowly evolve beyond them. They help them remove the parts of the design that alter or prevent growth. These practitioners also know about the deeper aspects of a person's life that tend to block progress—the snags that have been left in place for far too long. In essence, a soul-healing professional guides a person in reweaving their tapestry to get them not only on a better human path, but also the route that much better aligns with their soul.

I use this metaphor to help clients understand that even mental health concerns are part of their overall story. What they can learn about themselves and their struggles always informs them about how to evolve—how to go about changing the fabric of their life. Weaving is a meticulous process and requires time and energy to master, particularly when life continues to throw challenging events our way. This metaphor gives people an understanding that healing is a process, one that might require various skills and methods as they redesign and reweave their tapestry. The image empowers people to become the artisan of their life.

Existential Therapy

Existential Therapy is an approach to psychotherapy that focuses on understanding the "whole" person, not just the symptoms the person experiences. While some say it is an approach rather than a modality, the existential perspective offers a wider understanding of who a person really is. Existentialism is based on the work of philosophers Friedrich Nietzsche and Soren Kierkegaard who both emphasized that the nature of being human is a central philosophical issue and when this philosophy is applied to therapy, the healing process expands.

The primary concepts presented by existential therapy include that 1) all individuals have the capacity for self-awareness, 2) each person has a unique identity, 3) people must continually re-create themselves because life's meaning constantly evolves and changes, and 4) anxiety is part of the human condition.

Existentially based therapists promote the idea that a person is more than the sum of his or her parts, emphasizing that anything other than whole person care will fall short. Because people operate under the assumption of having free will, existentialism encourages individuals to become master observers of their lives as they live with purpose, hold values and find meaning in the way they respond to and experience life.

Restated, existential therapy urges individuals to become more conscious of their soul story (tapestry of life), understand that their soul is unique, embrace the opportunity (through free will) to reweave their pattern and accept that anxiety is something to understand as part of their soul's journey. As individuals realize there are ways to address their concerns through body, mind and soul, they become more whole. Yes, this is a bit of a romanticized image of anxiety-related disorders, but it offers an individual both an explanation for why their anxiety exists and empowerment for overcoming their suffering.

With this in mind, perhaps it is time to look at health and healing from a wider lens. By expanding the view of the loom, we can understand that to weave a healthy tapestry of life, all factors of life need attention. In doing so, we can start to look at anxiety and other mental health concerns in a more holistic way; we can include all aspects of a person's experience into treatment—body, mind and soul.

Only then will the real healing begin.

Anxiety and The Tapestry of Life

Few who suffer from anxiety would deny that something keeps "snagging" them when anxious moments arise, something even deeper than what medication or traditional therapy have managed and addressed. The very essence of who they are knows that something is still amiss. As existential therapists would agree, a person can learn to minimize and sometimes ignore the symptoms that come with anxiety, but the meaning behind the experience should be discovered in order to resolve the core issue.

Many soul-based factors may impact the experience of anxiety in a person's life. Epigenetic influence, generational experiences, ancestral trauma, past-life trauma, life lessons, age of a person's soul, astrological personality and more could play a role. Much more about each of these will be addressed in the chapters to come. Examples of work with my own clients will be included to help illustrate how these factors may impact conceptualization and treatment of anxiety through a whole person—and a whole soul view.

While full resolution of anxiety reactions is not promised by reading this book, a wider and deeper lens is offered to assist in answering what additional factors might play a part.

From a personal perspective, I've come to very much appreciate my own experience of healing and soul evolution at the intellectual, emotional and soul level as part of my individual tapestry of life. Because I've faced many difficult life events—a tragic accident of a parent at age nine and subsequent death at age twenty-one, sexual trauma during teenage years, a challenging marriage and divorce, serious mental health issues in both my immediate and extended family, graduate training (extremely stressful in itself!), several moves around the country, job stress, sexual harassment by a colleague, difficult family dynamics, business ownership, a few health scares, stressful and heavy experiences during the pandemic, and more—I can appreciate how complicated the human condition can become. As I've come to understand the idea of a "soul path" through the tapestry of life, laced with life lessons with spiritual underpinnings, this concept has played a huge role in how I work with clients. Often it is the soul-based explanation that starts a person on a better and richer path to healing.

The remainder of this book is dedicated to exploring the many soul factors that may impact the experience of anxiety and related disorders. My mission is to share these in such a way that a bridge will be built between traditional and soul-based healing. My intention is to show how all treatment methods are helpful and/or sometimes necessary to fully address a person's concerns.

PART TWO
THE SOUL SIDE OF ANXIETY

Give me the beauty in the inward soul, And may the inward and outer be at one.

SOCRATES

CHAPTER SEVEN

THE EVOLUTION OF SOUL HEALING

*A true healer is one who heals himself first
so others can benefit from his own healing.*
HONG CURLEY

I've shared the evolution of both body and mind practices in the treatment of anxiety and other mental health disorders in the previous chapters. The remainder of the book will explore the less-known practices of soul healing. First, a little information about how spiritual healing first began.

Origins of Spiritual Healing Around the World

The spiritual practice of healing existed long before modern medicine became an organized field. In fact, an ancient proverb, "Physician, heal thyself" has origins prior to the Christian Bible and was quoted in the Gospel of Luke (4:23).

The first spiritual healers may date back as far as 30,000+ years according to ancient artwork still visible on walls of caves and cliffs. Paleolithic art from 25,000 years ago showed images depicting shamanistic practices. Shamanism is a spiritual practice in which a practitioner uses altered states of consciousness to interact with the Spirit world for the sake of healing people, land or processes of nature. True shamans don't decide they want to practice the art of healing, they are chosen by clans or tribes because of their inherent spiritual gifts.

The first healing centers were actually temples (ancient Greece) and monks and priests ran subsequent healing establishments, many in churches where religious services were performed. Even the word "healer" is typically only used outside of hospitals, predominantly in spiritually based forums.

Currently, while nearly eighty-five percent of individuals wished spirituality was discussed during appointments with medical providers, less than ten percent even report the mention of prayer or other spiritual concepts. As you will see, many forms of soul healing already exist, with millions seeking these services regardless of whether their medical providers know their patients are involved in these healing modalities. Modern medical practices that treat anxiety and other mental health concerns would greatly improve if the soul—the essence of who an individual is—was factored into treatment.

While modern providers need not be chosen by a clan or tribe to provide soul healing, the decision to understand the importance of the soul in the treatment of mental illness will no doubt facilitate and accelerate healing.

Evolution as a Spiritual Psychologist and Soul-Healing Specialist

It's hard for me to pinpoint when my spiritual journey began. I grew up in a Catholic household and loved the rituals included in Sunday church services—the singing, kneeling, praying, and greeting of others. I loved the scent of incense burning, the sound of the organ playing and the shadows that fell on the stained glass windows. To be honest, I didn't really listen to the sermons and found myself tuning out to enter a very quiet-minded state as the priest spoke. I realize now that I was likely meditating, knowing I "went" somewhere each Sunday—I just didn't know where that place was. All I knew was that I returned feeling very peaceful and content.

My first intuitive memory was about a "weird" experience I had when I was in middle school. I remember looking at a bottle of nail polish and thinking, "That's going to tip over." About a minute later, it fell over without a nudge of the table it was sitting on. At the time, I didn't really think anything about it, chalking it up to an odd coincidence.

Several other unusual incidents happened in between, but the next notable events occurred as my father lay dying in the hospital when I was twenty-one years old. The day we knew his body was failing, I "saw" his soul for the first time. He had been placed on a ventilator sixteen days prior due to extreme emphysema and lung failure, which also accompanied heart and kidney malfunction. I stood by the hospital bed as the priest entered to give him his last Catholic rites. My father turned to look at me with terror in his eyes as the awareness of his passing suddenly sunk in. I vividly remember the moment our eyes met because I completely understood what he was experiencing in that moment—disbelief, shock and terror—and yet, relief that his fight was soon over. His life journey had come to an end.

Later that day, he had already entered a coma when we were told to go home to rest because the medical staff didn't know how long it would take for him to slip away. That was Christmas Day of 1990. As stunned as we all were at his pending transition, we all eventually went to bed. I woke after a profound dream. I dreamt I was sitting in a conference room talking to my father when the lights suddenly went out, issuing in pure darkness and no sound. In the dream, I called for my father but got no answer. As I realized I was awake, but sitting on the edge of the bed, the phone rang. It was the hospital calling to tell us he only had a few more minutes before he'd be gone. His time had come.

After I moved away to attend graduate school at age twenty-three, I experienced many days when I felt terrible from an emotional perspective—sad, stressed, depressed and even irritated at times. At first, I thought it was part of the adjustment to moving eight hundred miles away from home even though I was thrilled to be doing what I was meant to do. Soon, I realized the moods came on very suddenly and seemed to have a pattern. I started to realize that the feelings happened on particular days aligned with difficulties a sibling was having at home. Each Saturday, I'd call my mother to check in and she'd fill me in on the events. The timing was uncanny, but I realized I was experiencing empathic sympathy pains for my sister who was struggling at the time. I was tuned into her energy even from that far away.

During graduate school, a friend with whom I had a strong connection introduced me to energy work (Reiki). I later came to understand that this was a karmic connection from the past, even though no relationship occurred beyond friendship. With the experience of knowing this person, I understood the concept of energy, the power of using it to heal and how it connected to my resonance with the soul (picking up on my sibling's pain is one example).

When I moved to complete my pre-doctoral internship—the final year of clinical training, I dove into reading every spiritual book I could get my hands on. I had three weeks before starting the yearlong training and I remember doing nothing but reading, sleeping, walking a nearby trail and starting over again the next day. I finished nine books in just those first three weeks.

Just prior to moving for the internship, a cousin who lived in Indianapolis convinced me to see an intuitive counselor she knew. Although I didn't dismiss the possibility of hearing some interesting information, I didn't want to give the practitioner anything she could read through body language. I was determined to stay neutral. However, within five minutes, she had me in tears as she talked about specific details of my father's death that even my cousin didn't know. She went on to describe the events of the previous few years along with details of what was to come in the next few. She told me I'd be returning to school and although I firmly said there was no way that would happen given that I'd just completed a rigorous doctoral program, it did. Strangely enough, I was offered the opportunity to earn an M.S. in Public Health as part of my post-doctoral training—free of charge and included as part of the fellowship. I didn't have to do a thing to apply. I just had to say yes and do a bit of work (although most of my credits transferred from my Ph.D. program so it was even easier than expected). My best friend was the one who reminded me that the intuitive counselor said I'd be returning to school.

Since that time, this same practitioner has helped me understand many events in my life, including relationships with friends, family and lovers, as well as has guided me through many of my own life transitions. Now, twenty-seven years later, I consider this practitioner both a mentor and colleague. I still receive annual intuitive readings from her, mostly to hear her sweet and comforting voice and to get an update about how she is.

As a young professional who was committed to practicing what I preached, I dedicated myself to doing my own healing work both psychologically and as a soul. I took multiple classes in spiritual development, attended my first retreats and very much connected with nature as part of my evolutionary process. Travel became an essential part of my life and on most occasions, I visited places I felt drawn to go but didn't know why I was led to visit until I realized visiting these places was part of my ongoing soul evolution.

Soon after my father died, my best friend and I went to the Grand Canyon for the first time. She had lost her sister to Leukemia nine months before my dad's death and we both needed to get away. On our drive home she and I both noted how much more peaceful we felt by just absorbing the energy of the canyon. I now understand that I've had significant past lives in the area and I was simply being called "home" to heal. I've traveled there six times since, and rafted 277 miles through it the summer before writing this book. I refer to my time on the rafting trip, as a period of "rebirth" as I traveled down the river. The canyon metaphorically became a "birth canal" because I knew I was undergoing an extraordinarily intense and thorough spiritual upgrade at the time, one that has prompted the writing of this and other books for individuals to better understand the soul.

On my first trip to New Mexico to attend a conference in 2003, I heard the words, "You've been here before" as I saw the Sandia Mountain range. I cried, even though I wasn't sure what it meant at the time. Since then, many spontaneous past-life memories have surfaced. Many are related to places I've traveled, while others have helped me understand current relationships with people I knew in previous lives. Understanding past life experiences has helped me help others to heal much more thoroughly.

Around 2006, therapy clients started experiencing past-life images as memories, which emerged when I conducted deep visualization exercises. Healing took place as they remembered who they were previously, without my help in eliciting those responses. Luckily, I knew what was happening so I could explain and guide them in the next steps to healing. At other times, I found myself saying things to clients I couldn't have possibly known without them sharing details. Both my clients and I were often astounded. As time went on, I embraced the fact that my own intuition was building and came to understand that it helped clients when I shared my spiritual "hits". Each time I did, the clients' healing accelerated and resolution occurred much quicker.

As part of my own spiritual journey, I've been instructed by Spirit to visit certain countries without knowing why

(Peru—three times, Costa Rica, Bhutan, Nepal, Ireland to name a few, along with several seemingly random locations in the United States). All journeys provided spiritual awareness or awakenings that I now understand, even though I had no idea why I was supposed to visit those places before I went. Now if I get a nudge to go somewhere, I know something profound will occur. I don't try to figure it out ahead of time; I just let it unfold as part of my tapestry of life.

Over the years, I've studied numerous soul-healing modalities including energy work (Pranic Healing and Reiki), various forms of meditation and visualization, hypnotherapy, sound healing and vocal toning, crystal healing, the science of astrology, numerology and past-life regression therapy (with world-renowned psychiatrist, Dr. Brian Weiss), intuitive skills such as Akashic Records and Soul Realignment, ancestral healing techniques, shamanic and Native American healing strategies and more. I've read endless books by various well-known healers and have attended many spiritual conferences as well as have traveled to various spiritually based retreat or education centers. I've experienced shamanic soul-retrievals, karmic release ceremonies, Peruvian healing strategies, vision quests, energetic vortex tours and a myriad of different types of intuitive, sound and soul-healing sessions. I've spent time reading sacred texts as well as meeting with many spiritual leaders and healers, including monks in remote parts of Asia. I just can't get enough. Each time I experience something new, I understand more about the soul.

While I don't take spiritual work lightly, I tell people that I live somewhere between science and "woo". As a practitioner who was trained in traditional methods of science—both psychological (Ph.D. and M.S. in counseling psychology) and medical research (Master of Science in Public Health), I am versed in the importance of scientific discovery. As a healing practitioner, I have seen the power of soul-based strategies happen before my eyes, both in my own life and in nearly forty years of helping others. I've also seen where each traditional approach, when attempted alone, often fell short. My evolutionary path was paved so I could weave together my own tapestry of life in a way that I would illustrate to others how to go about their own healing process through body, mind and soul.

I don't claim to know everything about the soul and soul healing—I'm still learning something every day that helps me help others. However, I do know that it is beyond time to integrate traditional and spiritual methods of healing to reestablish whole person health but in a much more comprehensive way using both updated research and soul-healing strategies that are impossible to quantify. All aspects of healing hold value, whether focused on body, mind or soul. However, as it is said, the parts are not the sum of the whole. Individually, each approach simply stands alone. When offered together—or integrated into a fuller and richer approach to healing, amazing things can happen. True and complete healing becomes a possibility.

As described in the first section of this book, plenty of theory and research exists related to treating anxiety through the body and/or mind. Now it is time to bring the soul back to its rightful place in healing.

The Human vs. Soul Condition

The human condition has already been mentioned several times in this book. It is the unique and personal experience of an individual, including the good, the bad and the ugly parts of life. Scholars have striven to explain the many facets of our existence that impact day-to-day living, yet no one has attempted to comprehensively explain how the soul is involved.

The next chapter explores the idea of soul health and presents the model I created years ago to provide a visual understanding and roadmap for how to balance life, particularly after a challenging event. In this book, I more specifically list many possible ways anxiety plays a part.

The soul condition, or the many facets that influence how we operate and react as souls within our human condition, is explained more fully in the chapters that follow. Together, the human and soul conditions influence both our experience and ability to heal, whether from anxiety or any other mental or physical health concern.

CHAPTER EIGHT

SOUL HEALTH AND THE MANIFESTATION OF ANXIETY

The soul never thinks without a picture.
ARISTOTLE

Eighteen years ago, I contacted the graphic artist who worked with the web designer I had at the time. I asked her to create an image of a tree to depict the ten key aspects or "branches" I felt every person deals with throughout their experience of the human condition. I wanted to illustrate how every branch, including each leaf on it, interacts with the others to create "whole health".

At the time I started my Master's degree in Counseling Psychology, I also began a job as the Coordinator of Alcohol and Drug Education in the Student Health Promotion Department of the same university. It was a fortuitous position because I was introduced to the National Wellness Institute's (NWI) model of wellness (physical, psychological, social, intellectual, environmental, and spiritual health). While I was enrolled in a program to help people become mentally well, the classes seemed to only focus on pathology and illness. As I taught the NWI model to students and the community, I also started incorporating its concepts into what I learned as a blossoming therapist. Not only did I adopt the prototype, I adapted it. Over time, I realized that four obvious components were missing from the original model when it came to overall health; a person couldn't feel well and balanced unless each aspect was addressed.

I also came to understand that true healing was specific to the individual. Everyone's life—their tapestry—was different and as a result, their healing process was different as well. The essence of who a client is and what they had been through was present in every session. Their wounds uniquely seasoned and changed how they experienced life and this fact could not be ignored. Each client knew the discomfort or pain they felt altered their sense of self or identity—it misaligned them in such a way that they didn't know if they'd ever feel whole again.

What I originally called the "whole health model" soon became *The Soul Health Model*™. The essence of who a person is, wounds included, influences not only our ability to feel well, but also how we go about healing. My model of health had to include these factors.

I vividly remember the conversation I had with the graphic artist. I asked her to show movement in the image to indicate both support and growth from the trunk—the "soul" of the tree, as well as strength from within—the determination to both survive life's challenges and thrive beyond them. Because the soul is the core of who a person is and the branches—the ten key aspects of everyday life—create the "canopy" of health,

I needed the image to show the dynamic nature between all components. The artist nailed it.

SOUL HEALTH™ MODEL

As you can see, the ten essential elements of the human condition (Physical, Psychological, Social, Interpersonal, Intellectual/Occupational, Environmental, Financial, Spiritual, Sexual and Recreational) are the keys to balancing our everyday human lives—the health of each is essential in creating our overall sense of well-being and health. The interplay between these branches and factors affecting the soul illustrates why emotional concerns such as anxiety can be so complex. Blockage or misalignment of just one of these elements can prevent us from feeling whole, and because emotional conditions can be created by a complexity of factors, the model helps to illustrate why it is sometimes difficult to pin the origin down. Identifying which branch or branches are out of balance, wounded or damaged can take time to discover. However, this model serves as a map or blueprint to uncover the core issue(s) more quickly. It also serves as a tool to remind you of what needs to be healed or rebalanced throughout life.

Often, individuals feel completely worn and weary by their struggles, but *The Soul Health Model*™ introduces the vision of what life can be like once the key aspects of their lives are realigned.

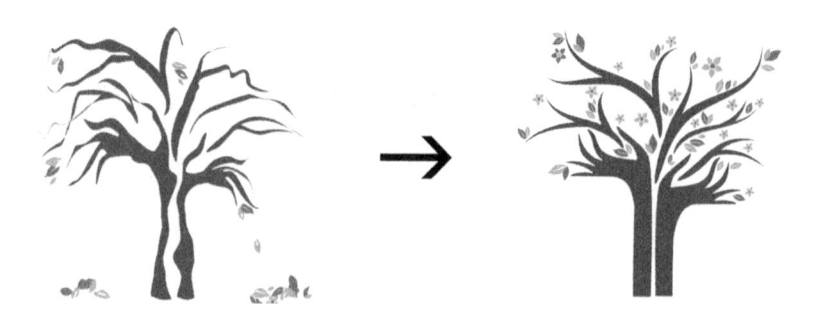

I've used the model in all aspects of my psychotherapy and soul healing work with clients, but also in my experience as a speaker in medical/mental health settings, continuing education workshops, corporate health environments and public venues. I offer the model as an educational tool to help others understand the interconnectedness of all branches, which helps people reconceptualize their "holistic" approach to healing. By understanding this model, it is impossible to overlook even one aspect of overall health while expecting to feel fully balanced. It just doesn't work.

The Ten Key Components of Health

Before exploring deeper soul factors that additionally impact anxiety, I will first explain each branch of health from the perspective of what we might experience as part of our human condition. As discussed earlier, keep *The Three Levels of Healing* in mind as you read through the descriptions of each branch. This will help you understand the depth of healing that might be necessary to feel whole again.

Each branch of health represents a key element of our existence as humans that affects our overall well-being. Specific to anxiety, various experiences related to each of the branches might influence how a person's unique manifestation of the disorder might have occurred. As I describe each branch below, I also list several possible examples of situations or circumstances that might contribute to anxiety-induced reactions.

It should be noted that misalignment or disturbance within each branch can result from distressing events in this lifetime or those prior. Also, depending on the severity of the event or wounding, misalignment can extend to the soul level even from events in just this lifetime, creating energetic imprints that are difficult to remove or resolve by traditional methods alone.

For a more in-depth look at the model, it may be helpful to read my book, *Soul Health: Aligning with Spirit for Radiant Living*. This book includes much more information about each branch as well as offers many exercises to assist in identifying aspects of health that need attention. Here, I will only provide a brief explanation of each branch, with possible connections to anxiety-related origins interconnected with how we experience the human condition.

Physical Health is defined as freedom from physical disease or other signs of ill health. Physical health is what most think of when asked about how healthy they feel in general. Healthy maintenance of this branch includes typical forms of self-care such as good nutrition, adequate sleep, basic physical fitness, reasonable mobility, adequate energy, and overall motivation.

Possible physical health-related connections to anxiety:

- Biochemistry (whether stress, health or genetically based)
- Genetics (having a genetic predisposition to anxiety and related disorders)
- Epigenetics (carrying generational emotional patterning simply due to DNA)
- Brain formation following early trauma (changes in brain structure)
- Health anxiety (real or imagined concerns/fears about the state of health)
- Trauma with injury (stress-induced reactions related to accidents or injury)
- Trauma from medical mishaps (anxiety-induced reaction due to an unexpected outcome)
- Drug/medication-induced anxiety (medical substances that disturb or don't match DNA) These may include: medications that include caffeine, some weight loss medications, birth control pills, cough/congestion medications

- Nutrition/vitamin deficiencies (as discussed in Chapter Five)
- Alcohol/substance use (reactions to use, overuse or abuse of substances)
- Cardiac/heart issues (chemical and neurological imbalances that follow)
- Thyroid issues (due to malfunction or imbalances)
- Sleep issues (sleep disorders as well as physically related pain, etc.)
- Blood sugar fluctuation (endocrine issues due to insulin resistance or skipping meals)
- Emotional eating behavior ("soothing" with food to cope with anxiety)
- "White Coat Syndrome" (fear of medical practitioners and procedures)

While physical aspects usually come to mind when we think of health, the nine branches that follow are equally important in experiencing overall well-being.

Psychological Health can be described as experiencing freedom from emotional *dis*-ease and the ability to maintain a sense of contentment. A healthy psychological branch of health includes an overall sense of well-being, self-esteem, positive self-image, and of course emotional health—including reasonable management of mental health concerns and psychological disturbances. This branch also accounts for our *perception* related to the health of the rest of the tree and how balanced our lives really are.

Possible psychological health-related connections to anxiety:

- Co-occurring mental health issues (depression, OCD, PTSD, Personality Disorders, etc.)
- Mental programming (parental style, early stress)
- Unusually high levels of stress (whether chronic or acute)
- Vigilance (fight or flight reactions)
- Sleep issues (inability to "turn off" thoughts, nightmares, etc.)
- Excessive worry (whether inherent or "trained" by caregivers)
- A general sense of lack of control (could stem from various circumstances or trauma)
- Generalized uncertainty (confidence issues, difficulty concentrating, etc.)
- Fear of change (personality-based or past negative experiences)
- Abuse as a child (sense of general instability and insecurity)
- Loss of loved one/parent (sense of being alone or without support)
- Negative thinking (self-defeating thought patterns)
- Personal triggers (smells, sounds, songs, places related to traumatic events)

Social Health refers to the other "beings" with whom we interact. These may include family, friends, partners, pets, neighbors, co-workers, clergy and other individuals with whom we have even peripheral contact. For some, having contact with others may actually create anxiety, making interactions quite difficult.

Possible social health-related connections to anxiety:

- Social anxiety (fear of critical evaluation, persecution or just being seen)
- Fear of intimate relationships (inability to create or foster close, meaningful connections)
- Attachment disorders (anxious, avoidant, ambivalent)
- Separation anxiety (fear of loss of significant contact, fear of being alone)
- Loneliness/isolation (real or imagined separation from others)
- Fear of authority (negative interactions with those perceived to be in power)
- Impact of introversion/extroversion
- Reactions to bullying (real or imagined distress)
- Social exclusion (isolation, abandonment or anxiety)

Interpersonal Health is separated from the Social branch to emphasize that this aspect of health reflects the *quality* of the relationships we share with others. Interpersonal health includes healthy boundaries, good communication, a good balance of independence and inter-dependence with others (strong give-and-take relationships), mutual respect, and equality within one's relationships. While we may have many social contacts in our life, it is the quality of these relationships that makes the difference in whether we feel healthy.

Possible interpersonal health-related connections to anxiety:

- Anxiety related to asserting self with others (controlling, narcissistic parent)
- Boundary issues (uncertainty of personal and other boundaries)
- Difficulty communicating needs (previously diminished by others)
- Racism (various anxiety-based responses related to racial bias, abuse, etc.)
- Harassment (worry about being fired or being forced into undesirable situations)
- Sexism (concern about gender inequality and impact on job, home life, etc.)
- Ageism (age-related anxiety, being treated differently, losing capabilities)
- Conflict (hard-wired fear of conflictual situations based on past experiences)

Intellectual/Occupational Health highlights the need for mental stimulation regardless of whether a person is gainfully employed. Intellectual challenge and genuine interest ensure a healthy branch, while engagement in daily tasks, curiosity about people and ideas, acquisition of new knowledge, and a general quest for learning also enhance our overall health.

Possible intellectual/occupational health-related connections to anxiety:

- Excessive fear of being laid off/fired (corporate downsizing/performance issues)
- Career confusion (extreme dissatisfaction and/or misalignment of career with lifestyle needs)
- Confidence (general lack of confidence or sense of agency in work environment)
- Imposter Syndrome (generalized sense that skills don't meet expectations)
- Performance anxiety (unreasonable expectations for job or workplace)
- Social Anxiety (impact on ability to perform well at work)
- Acquisitions/mergers (impact of cut-throat corporate culture)
- Retirement (anxiety about loss of identity, fear of losing viability in society)
- Fear of authority (anxiety related to unhealthy/toxic leadership)
- Study/test anxiety (fear of test performance, failure to progress in career path)

- Long working hours (impact of unreasonable workload on anxious person)
- Memory issues (declining cognitive processing)

Environmental Health depends on whether we live in clean, safe, healthy, and generally satisfying surroundings. It also includes a comfortable climate, good air quality, reasonable sound regulation, lack of clutter, and some degree of control over other external factors that might undermine our health and well-being. Environmental health also includes aspects of the "emotional environment" such as ongoing work stress, family tension, and threats to personal safety.

Possible environmental health-related connections to anxiety:

- Domestic violence/abuse (constant anxiety about home environment)
- Embarrassment about living conditions (difficult family member or fear of evaluation from others due to state of home/homelessness)
- Fear of large places (Agoraphobia, real or imagined concern based on trauma)
- Fear of small places (Claustrophobia, real or imagined concern based on trauma)
- Displacement (concern for losing home, unwanted move, actual loss of home)
- Natural disasters (anxiety induced by weather patterns/events based on previous traumatic experiences)

- Climate or "eco" anxiety (deep concern for how climate change will impact ability to live comfortably or sustainably)
- Fires and other tragic events (real or imagined concern)
- Housing issues/Homelessness (financial or other stress/anxiety related to loss)
- Hoarding behavior (fear-based acquisition of material items, loss-related)

Financial Health relates to having ample financial resources to meet our basic needs. This could include spending within our limits, preventing major debt, saving for the future, investing well, planning for retirement, and developing and maintaining healthy ideas about the use of money. Our beliefs about wealth and abundance also play a part in the vitality of this branch. In times of financial crisis, this branch can cause a tremendous impact on every other branch of health and cause great stress and/or anxiety.

Possible financial health-related connections to anxiety:

- Excessive worry about money (real or imagined fear of low resources)
- Fear of having money (real or imagined fear of having and managing resources)
- Poverty mindset (fear of identity changing by making more or less money than previously)

- Sudden expenses (acute anxiety/stress related to sudden job loss, big expenses including health problems, medical bills, etc.)
- Excessive spending (coping with stress by purchasing unnecessary goods)
- Worry about retirement (fear of having enough, expensive medical issues, etc.)
- Stock market crashes (anxiety responses to external causes)
- Lifestyle-induced financial stress (divorce, lawsuits, etc.)

Spiritual Health requires that we hold active and deliberate attention to our spiritual life for both growth and overall health. This can be reflected by a sense of inner peace and/or a belief in higher power. Having a healthy spiritual branch doesn't always include the practice of a formalized religion; instead, it might include regular participation in "centering" techniques such as prayer, meditation, and ritual.

Possible spiritual health-related connections to anxiety:

- "Church hurt" (anxiety related to rigid beliefs instilled while young, betrayal or abuse by religious authority or church members)
- "God Trauma" (sudden loss in belief, disillusionment in religious establishments)
- Fear of hell (deep belief of hellish conditions after life ceases)

- Fear of sin (intense fear of doing something unforgivable)
- Fear of death (anxiety about ceasing to exist)
- Cult-related experiences (either while a child or adult)
- Fear of no belief in higher power (unanswered questions about mortality, etc.)

Sexual Health is generally omitted from other wellness models, but often plays a key role in overall well-being. This element of health includes healthy sexual boundaries and an understanding of appropriate sexual activity with self and others. Sexual trauma is a great source of anxiety for many. The health of this branch emphasizes that a person sees sexual activity as an intimate act of relationship, not simply a way to fill basic, individual needs.

Possible sexual health-related connections to anxiety:

- Sexual anxiety (fear of sex, intimacy, pleasure due to rape, abuse and/or assault, fear of getting pregnant)
- Performance anxiety (anxiety-induced inability to perform or reach climax)
- Health anxiety (fear of contracting a sexually-transmitted disease or other illness)
- Hyperarousal (intense need for sexual release, often used as outlet for stress or anxiety)
- Fetishes (unusual sexual arousal to objects or situations, often originated from past trauma)

- Body image (deep discomfort with body, particularly when engaging in sexual activity, whether or not past trauma exists)
- Religious programming (anxiety about premarital sex/masturbation being a sin)
- Hormonal issues (both men and women can experience hormonal imbalances that could contribute to anxiety)

Recreational Health is often seen as an unimportant part of overall health despite the fact that leisure activities are shown to help us relax and decompress from everyday stress. Laughter and lightheartedness provide both physical and emotional release of tension, thus decreasing both stress and anxiety.

Possible recreational health-related connections to anxiety:

- Fear of leisure (Type A personality and other personality factors)
- Difficulty relaxing (anxious responses when physically slowing down or not actively engaging in activity, sometimes related to ADHD)
- Anxiety about appearing lazy (lack of self-worth, self-compassion, parental or societal programming)
- Fear of sweating (aversiveness to perspiration, fear of odor or appearance)
- Anxiety related to travel (fear of leaving home, fear of flying and other forms of transportation, etc.)

- Discomfort with discomfort (staying busy to avoid troublesome thoughts or emotions)
- Uncertainty about what is fun (anxious response to identifying needs)

As a reminder, the many examples above may simply seem like "human" concerns that were created by life events; although this is true, the impact of each may reach deep enough levels to fracture or alter the core of who a person is—their soul. Only soul-based methods will remove or resolve these issues while certain traditional methods may actually block or slow the healing process. However, ideally, methods that address the whole person—body, mind and soul—when combined is the best option.

It is also important to consider that two people who experienced the same stressful or traumatic event in this lifetime may still have completely different responses depending on their soul health prior to the event. This could be true due to several factors including previous trauma in this lifetime, trauma from past lives, certain life lessons a person is supposed to overcome, karmic situations in which a person needs to re-experience a similar trauma to heal or overcome a past life experience and so on. The more wounds a person already carries—either human or soul-based, the more susceptible a person is to more extreme responses. Many other soul-based factors might impact an individual's ability to resolve and heal from anxiety.

As described before, my own experience with anxiety stemmed from misalignment of several branches in my own life. The panic reaction during my unhealthy marriage no doubt stemmed from the social, interpersonal and environmental branches (the stressful home environment), along with stress related to graduate school (intellectual/occupational).

Later, when I experienced heart palpitations and intensely worrisome thoughts during the last two years of my mother's life, I could attribute them to imbalance in several branches: physical (I wasn't able to exercise as regularly due to frequent travel), psychological (stress and worry about my mother's health), social and interpersonal (pending loss and extremely challenging family dynamics), financial (lowered income due to time away as well as expenses of frequent travel), intellectual/occupational (I was also providing continuing education workshops around the country for a nationally-based company, which were enjoyable but also stressful in the midst of everything else), environmental (emotional environment of family dynamics), and recreational (I certainly had far less time for fun and leisure).

SOUL HEALTH™ MODEL

Luckily, being the author and designer of *The Soul Health Model*™, I knew what was out of balance and understood what I needed to do to feel better. I was also aware that my symptoms were simply signs from my soul that I needed to rebalance my life as soon as I was able. Once I had the time and energy to work on my branches of health, I felt healthy and well again.

In the midst of all of the stress, I became aware that several soul-based factors were playing a part in my life, each creating its own influence on my anxiety at the time. I will explain more about this in the chapters to come to help you understand that both human and soul-based influences affect both our experience of overall health and our ability to heal.

How to Use The Soul Health Model

There are endless ways to use *The Soul Health Model*™ as a blueprint or guide for either yourself or for those you serve. The model offers a comprehensive, "whole health" view at what we struggle with as part of being human. Related to anxiety, it may be most helpful to explore which branch or branches cause the most discomfort. Often one or more are interacting to produce immense unrest. However, keep in mind, as you work to improve one branch, the others are positively impacted as well.

The Soul Health Model™ displays what can happen to a person's overall experience if either a branch of the tree or the trunk is left unattended. Imbalance will inevitably occur. However, the model provides a visual cue to which branch or branches might need attention. Still, unless you know to look for deeper causes of disturbance, you might miss the cue to examine something deeper.

While each individual's tree looks different depending on which branch or branches need work, several additional factors influence everyone's experience of the human condition. These include individual life experiences, cultural influences, parenting and family of origin, gender, geographical location, genetic profile, societal norms, generational mindset, social programming, stage of life, political climate and the general level of consciousness or awareness a person holds. All of these factors influence how a person experiences mental health concerns as well as how—or if—they approach healing.

As you can see, whole health includes far more than the bio (body)- psycho (mind)- and social aspects of health. The ten key branches of the human condition must be addressed to understand what each individual needs from a human level in order to feel well or balanced. If you learn to utilize the needs of the soul to determine what you need in each branch, the balance and healing go much further.

By now, you are also starting to see that the soul side of health may play a part in overall coping and management of mental health conditions. Because anxiety is the most common mental health concern, it is reasonable to assume that many factors play a part in understanding the core of an individual's unique experience. As you learn more about the soul aspects that may be playing a part, you will more deeply understand the importance of identifying and addressing these issues.

For now, consider *The Soul Health Model*™ and explore how it currently fits and helps to explain the tapestry of your life.

Personalizing the information will help you understand the model much more. If you feel a more in-depth understanding of the model would be helpful, you may want to read *Soul Health: Aligning with Spirit for Radiant Living*.

CHAPTER NINE

UNDERSTANDING ANXIETY THROUGH THE SOUL SIDE OF HEALTH

*In your soul are infinitely precious things
that cannot be taken from you.*
OSCAR WILDE

Our mental health is a direct expression of how well we feel at a soul level. It is also a mirror for where we are in our evolutionary process. Most people think of Charles Darwin when considering evolution and only remember his early work that endorsed the idea of survival of the fittest—the assumption that those who are the strongest will outlive those who are more vulnerable in their ability to stay alive. The majority of people don't know that Darwin shifted his theory to say that it is those who adapt the best who seem to overcome the biggest challenges. This adaptation promotes healing while helping us to not only sustain life, but to thrive throughout it. It also helps us to evolve beyond previous obstacles, which resolves any challenges we might have previously had to overcoming them while also moving forward to live in a whole new way.

Similar to Darwin's updated version of the theory, it is those who learn to handle their mental health concerns from a broader perspective that seem to heal the most and find the most life satisfaction in the process. Those who dedicate themselves to learning about themselves seem to outgrow their once obstructive concerns and experience the most growth. Another form of evolution might be helpful in applying the concept of soul health.

Conscious Evolution

Conscious evolution refers to the ability of human beings to become sensible participants in their own personal growth and in the evolution of their cultures and/or society as a whole. It requires individuals to understand that they have ultimate choice in how their lives go and emphasizes the need to choose what is best for their ability to survive and thrive beyond simple physical means. To adopt a conscious view of life directly includes the commitment to adapt and change for the betterment of self, both for the sake of one's wellbeing and for how that bettered self tends to interact with and contribute to the world as a whole. In other words, if one person chooses to heal their concerns, it creates a positive impact on all those around that individual as well.

In the case of mental health concerns, especially the experience of anxiety, it is essential to take a conscious evolution approach to how you 1) understand your challenges (First Level of Healing), 2) manage, eliminate or dissolve both physical and emotional symptoms (Second Level of Healing) and 3) heal deep wounds that might exist and cause the disruption (Soul-Level Healing). All of these actions contribute greatly to not only your own quality of life but also to how you interact with all others as well. In other words, by stepping back to see your experience of the human condition from a much wider lens you can both facilitate and accelerate your ability to heal and thereby evolve.

I tell clients that it is not enough for me to help them heal. To me, healing means I am only interested in getting them back to where they once were. Instead, I want to help clients evolve beyond their concerns, moving past their challenges of the human condition as they heal. The more aware and conscious a person becomes about their experience within the human condition—including the symptoms and causes related to their anxiety and/or any other mental health concern—the more resolution of concerns can actually take place. I do not profess methods of symptom relief; I help clients capture the wisdom and knowledge about their inner ally that will eliminate disruption altogether.

Each individual has their own evolutionary path—their own tapestry of life. If viewed through the lens of conscious evolution, people would come to understand that many life challenges occur to stimulate growth for ourselves and/or for those around us. There is always something to be learned from each event that causes discomfort or disruption. By understanding this, a person often learns to use moment-to-moment awareness to rework their tapestry of life—to understand that the wounds held deep within are causing the disruption and understand the bigger picture of why their soul experiences deep discomfort. Each uprising of emotion, when seen through conscious eyes, informs an individual more about the wound that needs to be healed.

As mentioned already, our soul—our innermost self—tries to get our attention when something is amiss. Emotions alert us to the fact that something is misaligned in our lives that prevents us from feeling well, stable or whole. Unfortunately, because symptom relief is the first line of treatment in most traditional settings and very few practitioners know to use those symptoms as the true fodder for healing and growth, most people are left managing reactions rather than healing to the point of whole—or soul-level health. They don't know that understanding the discomfort from a deeper level leads them to the answers for why the disruption exists.

Anxiety is often a direct expression of our soul's plea for help. I've worked with hundreds of clients who never thought to explore the meaning behind their concerns; they just wanted to stop the discomfort. Until we explored their overall tapestry of life, whether formally or indirectly, their anxious reactions persisted. They kept being "snagged" by their emotions until they learned to honor and interpret them as part of deeper and wider healing. As mentioned previously, I emphasize to clients that often our mental health is not only a reflection of what is going on much deeper, but it is also an artifact of what we are supposed to learn and evolve beyond as we travel through life. Much meaning can be found in how everything is woven together, but often it takes the metaphors, explanations, dedication to engaging in the healing process, and willingness to evolve to fully resolve concerns to truly find whole health.

For example, some anxiety (such as generalized and excessive worry) is laced throughout life as part of an ongoing lesson to take things less seriously or learn to trust oneself and/or the process of living more. For others, anxiety might abruptly appear to get their attention about something that needs more urgent care, as in the case of an emerging panic disorder (which is what happened for me in alerting me of the need to leave an unhealthy marriage). The origin of some conditions may also lie in past lives and by discovering the details that created the first disruption; often a person captures the awareness about how it applies in the current lifetime.

Once dots are connected, an individual finds peace. But if the core reason anxiety exists is left unattended, discontent and disruption are sure to continue. While modern treatment of anxiety has answered some of the questions about how to manage symptoms, only the soul will illuminate what is really going on beneath the surface. Adopting the concept of conscious evolution will help you widen the lens in looking at your life to get to the bottom of what may cause your anxious reactions.

Other Human Factors and Anxiety

When I created *The Soul Health Model*™ so many years ago, my intention was to help people understand that all of the branches of the human condition worked together and that the soul—the essence of who we are—influenced each one throughout our human journey. The model helped people understand the complexity of elements that might impact any given form of mental unrest. It provided a blueprint or roadmap for how to realign a person's life to experience more peace. The soul's most natural state is joy and contentment, so the image allowed both patients and practitioners to quickly see what played a part in the imbalance.

Over the years, I realized that many additional "human factors" influence our steadiness within each branch and in our overall ability to experience whole health. Remember, the human condition is defined as the positive and negative aspects of being human. It encompasses all that humans do and experience within their lifetime, and simply put, is the way in which an individual lives and everything that entails. Yes, it's complex. And that is why a thorough understanding of anxiety—which is also quite complex—is necessary to both get to the bottom of what caused it and how to fully evolve beyond your experience of it.

The human factors I list below come from outside of us but impact us deeply at the soul level. The individual essence of who we are is inevitably laced and influenced by what happens around us. Therefore, we must look both outside ourselves and deeply within to fully comprehend who we are and who we have become at a soul level as a result. Factors of the human condition add layers to each branch and to our overall experience of health.

Below, I briefly explain each factor so your awareness about how each may have contributed to the overall experience of anxiety may be illuminated. Keep in mind that the soul is the essence of who we are. Every experience we have either seasons or scars us as we travel through the human condition, whether in this lifetime or any prior. Because everything is energy, the radiance of our life force depends entirely on whether we heal from whatever wounds or harms us. Aligning and balancing our branches of life includes healing both internal and external factors that affect daily living.

Life Experiences

No one experiences the exact same path through life. As a soul, each individual already holds their own perspective and ability to navigate the many ups and downs of the human condition. If an individual experiences anxiety-provoking events at any time in life—including in the womb if the mother's life is already stressful—it will directly impact the essence of who we are. This may seem obvious, but taken in context, most medical (body-based) treatment for anxiety only addresses the symptoms, not the origin of how or why they began. Some mind-based treatments are the same, only addressing how to manage anxious thoughts and emotions, not what caused them in the first place.

Trauma

Trauma—a deeply distressing or disturbing experience—is the most common factor that creates an experience of anxiety. Many think of trauma as something that is catastrophic in nature, but depending on the individual, their experience of life, their life lessons and human- and soul- factors may all play a part in whether an individual experiences, manages or heals anxiety. Various trauma-based therapies have been developed and even trauma-informed educational practices are now becoming popular in schools to assist in individual student needs.

Self-Aspects

As you're learning, the true essence of who we are is at the core of all of the ways we experience life. Self-aspects can include the different "parts" of who we are, whether fragmented by trauma, our different roles we play throughout life, how fully we express who we are, etc. When it comes to anxiety, our sense of self or our ability to experience an integrated identity can have a direct impact on any of the branches depicted in the *Soul Health Model*™. Anxiety may or may not impact each one depending on whether that part of our overall health is wounded or misaligned.

Cultural Influences

Culture plays a significant role in whether a person experiences anxiety because of the unique influences it plays in a person's life. It also plays a part in whether it is socially acceptable within that culture to seek assistance in healing. Unfortunately, the nuances of the impact of treating those with cultural influences have not been flushed out enough. Here, just know that it plays a noteworthy role in both human- and soul-based healing. Differing cultural values may play a part in whether individuals seek body, mind or soul-based services for anxiety-related conditions.

Parenting/Family of Origin Dynamics

The experience of anxiety often stems from how caregivers impacted an individual from an early stage of life. Whether passed down genetically, through modeling anxious reactions to everyday events, or by creating anxiety through poor parenting, abuse or inability to properly care for an individual at a young age in some other way, anxiety can affect the essence of who an individual is just by the circumstances into which they were born.

Gender Aspects

You may not initially think that gender can play a role in the experience of anxiety, but the deep seated expectations of males and females can easily influence how a person experiences life. Each gender inherently holds responsibility within a family, culture, society and the world in general. While gender roles are changing as modern societies evolve, this evolution causes additional stress as expectations and roles readjust. Also, as various aspects of gender identity shift, anxiety can play a part. Gender is deeply connected to the essence of who we are and whether gender-related human- or soul-factors are involved, anxiety can result.

Geographical Location

Where a person lives can also influence the experience of anxiety. Urban vs. rural, state to state, country to country, continent to continent, ocean to mountains, climate to climate, and many other factors are part of any geographical influence on a person's human condition and soul. Even location can have a culture that creates various life experiences based on where a person lives. Understanding anxiety often entails recognizing the influences of the place in which a person lives.

Genetic Impact

While it might not be immediately apparent how genetics impacts various branches of the *Soul Health Model*™, the overall experience of health and well-being may be influenced by the inherited profile of an individual. Obviously, heredity can play a part in the physical (body) and psychological (mind) aspects of treating anxiety. When you expand the view, you will be able to see that all aspects of well-being may be influenced. For example, genetics plays a part in intellectual health (intelligence and cognitive ability), sexual health (hormones), and interpersonal health (personality characteristics).

Societal Norms

Society directly impacts our experience of anxiety, especially depending on how particular values influence individuals. A high-stress society instills expectations that are often unrealistic or unhealthy in general. Also, highly restrictive or controlled societies don't allow an individual to express their true essence, which can cause disruption in their ability to enjoy and balance life. While some nations consciously work on accepting a variety of ideas and values, resistance to change often contributes to an individual's ability to either manage their anxiety or heal beyond it.

Generational Mindset

Each generation holds certain ideas and values, but as the world evolves these may no longer fit. For those whose values simply don't fit the generation in which they are reared, anxiety can result. Humans are communal beings and want to belong. When generational thoughts and values change, it can be difficult to feel you have support. Remember, the essence of who we are wants to be free enough to live in alignment with our soul's needs and desires. When a soul's evolution depends upon their ability to be authentic, any misalignment or barrier to this can create disruption.

Social Programming/Constructs

Whether programmed by parenting or by other societal factors, it is not uncommon to experience distress as we outgrow or evolve beyond constructs that no longer serve us. The very concept of evolution entails shifting with the times. Many things impact social constructs, including how research reveals new data about what is or isn't good for a person's mental health, how our mental health directly impacts thoughts, behaviors and emotions as part of quality of life and also which values are simply outdated given where we are today. Both resistance to changing ideas and the disturbance of a slow-to-change world can create anxious reactions in some.

Epigenetic Imprint

While our genes play a significant role in our health, epigenetics is the study of how our behaviors and environment also affect the manner in which our genes respond and work. A fairly new field, epigenetics explores how our DNA "turns on and off" according to factors such as an individual's physical development, age, impact of environment, experience of illness, etc. Related to mental health, epigenetic influence also plays a role in anxiety. While parents or other extended family members may not hold specific genetic markers for certain mental health concerns, offspring can become more vulnerable (their genes may "turn on") to experience anxiety if their ancestors experienced intense or extended stress. In this way, a family history of a diagnosable mental health condition may not be relevant. Anxiety then can contain an epigenetic imprint that could contribute to an individual's experience of the condition.

Stage of Life

The human condition provides many stages in which both stress and anxiety are more likely. Simply put, being human just isn't easy. Depending on the stage of life a person is in; various factors could contribute to create anxiety-related experiences. More anxiety is likely during key junctures in human development and impacts us as a result of the transition between stages, depending on how that particular human adjusts. For instance, adolescent years, retirement and issues with aging can all create heightened anxious reactions. Some of this comes from the biological impact during that stage of life while the stress of transitioning may be enough to make a person anxious. Regardless, stage of life is important to consider as a key factor in the experience of anxiety.

Natural Disasters

Much anxiety is experienced because those suffering don't or haven't felt in control for one reason of another. There is very little that can be controlled in predicting when a disastrous event will occur or how it will impact any given individual. While some people fear that a disaster will happen—some without seeming cause—many who have experienced a serious natural event become anxious that another one will come along to even more deeply affect their lives. In many cases, natural disasters impact all branches of *The Soul Health Model*™, so it makes sense that an individual's deepest essence—their soul—will be affected.

World Events

Whether directly impacted or not, many individuals experience anxiety as a result of knowing a world event has occurred. Perhaps this stems from deep compassion for individuals who experience war and/or other tragedy or sometimes events that occur on the other side of the world trigger an individual's anxiety for other reasons. Regardless, the collective anxious energy of such situations can deeply alter an individual's ability to cope in their own human condition. The 2020 COVID-19 pandemic is a very recent example of how a world event can rapidly increase widespread anxiety.

Political Climate

There's nothing like political strife to stir worry about safety, security and the state of a country or world. As a psychologist, it is not unusual for me to spend many hours each day working with clients to calm uncertainty when political tension is high. People's anxiety can be triggered by economic concerns, fear of war, conflict between loved ones and more. This is a prime and relevant example of how much the energy of something outside of us can so strongly impact who we are deep within.

Core Motivators

Numerous personality inventories or paradigms explore what makes people tick. Anything from work style (Myers-Briggs Personality Test), self-awareness (Big 5 Personality Test, Sociotype), interpersonal profile (Interpersonal Communications Skills Test, Enneagram), emotional intelligence (Berkeley Emotional

Intelligence Test, Verywell Mind), personal strengths (Character Strengths Survey, Strength Finders), sensitivity to others (Empathy Quotient), career path (Human Metrics, Career Hunter) and many more attempt to explain a person's core motivations. While these tests don't directly identify links to anxiety, when taken in context, it is easy to see why certain core motivations can impact an individual's experience of the condition if locked into patterns that make coping difficult.

Capacity for Love/Self-Love

The ability to love and accept oneself is essential in any healing process. In fact, sustainable change only happens when we care enough about ourselves to permanently alter our lives for the sake of our overall health. However, given the many ways the human condition distracts us or attempts to pull us out of alignment, self-love remains perhaps the toughest lesson we are faced with as we learn to navigate life. Similarly important is the capacity to love others and let others love us. Both are necessary aspects of overcoming the challenges of the human condition. When it comes to anxiety, many people struggle with self-loving thoughts when anxiety-provoking moments overtake them.

Bioenergetic Field

Less known in mainstream health, the bioenergetic field of a human body contains several levels of energy that impact an individual's health. In holistic health, the human energy field is often referred to as the subtle body—the invisible energetic fields that surround the body and affect it on many levels. They are depicted as layers or conjoined fields of electromagnetic energy around the body and include four primary levels of energy: Bioplasmic (the body), Emotional (feelings and emotional energy), Mental (thoughts, perceptions, cognitions) and Collective Consciousness (energetic connection with the external world). When healthy, energy flows freely between these levels, allowing us to feel centered, grounded and well. When blocked or disrupted, we can manifest various physical and emotional illnesses. In the case of anxiety, the energy within our biofield can become disturbed or blocked in such a way that it causes the experience of human anxiousness. Those who perform energy work on others recognize that imbalances in an individual's bioenergetic field must be realigned in order for healing to take place. For instance, those who unknowingly allow others' energy fields to impact their own can experience intense anxiety or other discomfort if sensitive to such exposure. With the essence of an individual in mind, if "invaded" by another's energy or if the layers of the biofield are out of alignment, the soul can suffer and mainstream treatment will not improve a person's well-being. As discussed in previous chapters, understanding energy and the energetic layers a person holds can be instrumental in healing from any anxiety-based disorder.

Level of Human Consciousness

While the study of mindfulness has been a part of mental health treatment for a few decades, consciousness is newer to the scene. Mindfulness implies moment-to-moment awareness of the good, bad and ugly parts of everyday life; consciousness indicates that an individual actively takes what they have become mindful about and inherently integrates this knowledge into how they think and behave as a result. In other words, the more conscious a person is about their situation, the more likely they are to take action to change something and also to be successful in doing it. Treatment of the body is not a very conscious process—the medication or treatment works to minimize the physical experience of anxiety. Some mind-related treatments focus on increasing awareness and assisting a person in managing and eliminating symptoms, but not all incorporate aspects of conscious action. For many to overcome anxiety, it is necessary for them increase their level of human consciousness to fully heal.

As you can see, both internally- and externally-created concerns impact our human condition. If anxiety is not relieved after exploring and healing from these concerns, you can be certain that additional factors apply. This is where the soul comes in.

Transpersonal Psychotherapy

No theory of psychology comprehensively includes all of the factors listed above as part of treatment, but Transpersonal Psychology—a less-known branch of the field—does aim to incorporate a wide array of ideas, disciplines and theories. Transpersonal psychologists use philosophy, art and literature, health theories, cognitive science and various spiritual traditions to explore the whole human experience. The field began in the late 1960s and was co-founded by psychologist, Abraham Maslow and psychiatrist, Stanislav Grof based on an integration of earlier works by none other than Carl Jung, the founding father of psychology who emphasized the importance of the soul. Transpersonal psychology is generally not included in traditional psychology degree programs, but it is advancing in popularity as key elements of spiritual psychology gain interest: higher potential, transcendence and the overall state of consciousness. Regardless of the slow growth of this part of the field, it is encouraging that more therapists are exploring the spiritual aspects of whole person health.

In the next chapter, I explain the many anxiety-related soul factors that might affect your experience of whole health.

CHAPTER TEN

HEALING THE ROOTS OF ANXIETY

Anxiety can act as internal gravity, shrinking the soul.
FREDRIK BACKMAN

When treating mental health concerns, many therapists ascribe to healing wounded "parts" of us to restore balance. In the 1920's Jacob and Zerka Moreno developed a creative way to solve problems and heal emotional wounds through psychodynamic theory, which holds the premise that aspects of us arise when role-played within a group. These "psychodramas" provided a dynamic way for many people to experience powerful healing at the same time. Although just one person serves as the "protagonist", the central character trying to solve a personal issue, the intended outcome is that people heal aspects of themselves through vicariously experiencing the roles enacted by others. During my early training, I experienced such groups and they are, in fact, quite powerful in illuminating different parts of oneself along with what comes to the surface as a result of simultaneously observing how they all work together to create one primary personality.

More recently, American family therapist, Richard Schwartz, developed Internal Family Systems (IFS) in the 1980's with the idea that our mind consists of relatively distinct subpersonalities based on how a person reacts to particular situations or events. He believed that each part held unique viewpoints and qualities and by identifying how they reacted, those parts could be healed and the mind would come back into balance from whatever emotional disturbance arose. Schwartz emphasized that each part has a positive aspect and the goal was not necessarily to eliminate the parts, but to harmonize them in a way to help them work together to bring the mind back into balance. He posited that in doing so, a person would be better able to access their true Self—the sense of an integrated identity. While identifying each part is an intellectual process, Schwartz noted that by creating a harmonious system between the parts, a person would reach a state of being that combined the mind, emotions and body. He talks about "self-energy", which is the experience one has when all parts are aligned.

Both theories focus on the integration of different aspects of the personality to become more whole, each offering powerful tools to manage the mind. However, neither reaches the depth of healing the deepest essence of who we are since the self and the soul are two separate parts of the same individual.

These theories lend much value in understanding the need to heal the various roles and parts of our existence and the concept can be easily applied to healing the body, mind and soul once people learn how to do so. *The Soul Health Model*™ helps you understand more thoroughly which parts (branches) of the human condition might need attention in order to rebalance and realign life. It also helps you see how each branch is influenced by the soul—the deep aspect that drives each thought, emotion and behavior. The additional human factors discussed in the last chapters help you see how many elements of the human condition influence and impact each branch.

When the branches of your human condition are aligned and in balance, your soul is more at peace. However, if your soul is wounded or damaged in ways you are unaware, it is difficult to balance the rest of life. Therefore, the soul and your human condition work in tandem to create the experience of the whole—one will not feel in balance if the other is not. Something will feel like it is missing or misaligned.

Soul Factors and Anxiety

I've become increasingly aware since I first created *The Soul Health Model*™ that many more factors, which operate under the surface, need to be brought to light. Over time, I developed an expanded version of the model to illustrate how additional influences affect everyone's experience of the human condition as well as the many factors that affect the soul. It was necessary to add "roots" to the tree to help people more fully understand their deeper aspects.

The roots of the tree depict the many facets of the soul that are less known to the general public. Although a book could be written on each factor itself, I will take the time here to simply define and briefly explain each one. Bear in mind that many of these aspects will be unfamiliar to you until you learn more about how they impact your life. Remember, the soul has been left out of healing since the very first years in which the field of medicine was formed. Much has been forgotten or ignored in the path of healing and nowhere have these factors been previously assembled to illustrate the complexity of our human experience. It is time to bring these concepts back to light in one cohesive model.

THE SOUL CONDITION

While I briefly describe each factor, I intentionally emphasize those most related to anxiety-related disorders. In the last chapter, you saw how the branches of the *Soul Health Model*™ might be directly affected by these factors—you just might not have known what they were. I purposely provided examples of soul-based origins of anxiety prior to explaining which factor might apply to give you context in linking the human and soul-based factors that might exist. I've done this both to help you visualize how each branch may be influenced by more than the human condition and to ease you into understanding the depth at which the soul may play a part in the experience of anxiety-related illness.

To many, this way of understanding human life and anxiety, in particular, will be new. However, once your conceptualization expands, it will all likely make sense. Take your time exploring the many possible factors that contribute to anxiety as you gain more understanding about how body, mind and soul intersect to create the true essence of whom a person is.

Soul Consciousness

Similar to the level of human consciousness discussed in the last chapter, the level of soul consciousness also plays a part. Just by reading this book, you are expanding your understanding about how the soul plays a significant role in overall human function and health. The more a person sees that the human condition is part of the soul's ongoing evolution and journey, the more the individual can learn to use their experiences to both heal and grow. The awareness that anxiety is often manifested from deeper causes and that the experience of it—once acknowledged as a catalyst for something to change—allows an individual to evolve beyond their circumstances and perhaps leave anxious responses behind. Numerous books and other resources about soul consciousness are now available and more are likely to come. None, to date, directly explain how consciousness is connected to specific mental health concerns.

Life Lessons

When approaching life using a wider lens, one can more consciously see that many of our trials and tribulations hold lessons. I often say that discomfort always accompanies evolution, meaning that most people don't change unless there is something making them uncomfortable enough to do so. We need a catalyst to put change into motion; otherwise, we tend to repeat patterns and routines with little alteration of behavior. All of my clients who struggle with anxiety are immediately taught to look at what they learn from their anxious symptoms—what their condition is trying to tell the client as part of stimulating growth. This empowers clients to take a more conscious and active role in changing their responses. Once an individual understands what they are supposed to learn so they can outgrow issues related to their anxiety, their discomfort diminishes and the symptoms either subside or vanish. From the soul level, there's something bigger our inner ally wants us to know and discomfort is often the only way to get our attention. Once a lesson is learned, we evolve beyond what once disrupted our lives.

Life Purpose

As mentioned multiple times in this book, the soul is the truest and deepest part of who we are. When we don't know who that is, we can feel anxious and none of our branches of life may feel aligned. Often the biggest misalignment stems from feeling unsure of one's true purpose in life. While we actually have many purposes throughout our lifetime—some simultaneously—the misalignment of one or more of our branches of health can make us feel far off from our soul's intended path. Also, when circumstances of our human condition don't allow us to live a purposeful life, our mental health can greatly suffer. In turn, our soul becomes restless and creates the experience of anxiety to attempt to further get our attention.

As a soul-healing specialist, many clients seek my services to help them understand what they are supposed to be doing to fulfill their purpose. For them, it feels like something is missing. These individuals know that in order to advance beyond their current level of soul evolution— "graduating" as they move into their next lifetime—they must identify what it is they are supposed to fulfill as they travel through the current life. Discomfort of all sorts lessens when a person finds their true path and anxiety, in particular, tends to dissipate.

Gender Heritage

While gender aspects were discussed as part of the human factors in the previous chapter, gender heritage is different. Each soul has a gender, one that influences the human part of them throughout lifetime. An individual can have a male soul in either a male or female body in this lifetime or a female soul in either as well. In many ways, the heritage of the soul's gender directly impacts how one experiences life. For instance, part of what I do in certain soul-healing sessions is help a person understand how many lifetimes they've lived as males vs. females in the past. This immediately affirms why a person may be confused by the roles they've played, the skills they inherently possess or how others perceive them. It is not unusual to see a female who has many inherent skills that might appear to be more masculine in nature. It is also common to see a male who holds a more feminine role or demeanor. A person who identifies more closely to the gender they've been most often in previous incarnations can explain the growing number of transgender identities. However, without this awareness within soul consciousness, great anxiety and discomfort can exist in figuring out whom a person truly is and how they want to live in this lifetime. Also, without this understanding, individuals can be condemned and wronged just because they are trying to live more authentically as the soul gender they really are. This is a difficult concept to grasp, but one that makes sense given the circumstances mentioned above.

Soul Age

Many can describe what an old soul is without ever thinking about what it really means. An old soul is someone who seems to be beyond their years in maturity, wisdom and understanding of the world in general, despite their young chronological age. When it comes to the soul, there are, in fact different "ages" according to how long that soul has lived (how many lifetimes they have experienced). A person could be an old soul in a young body or a young soul in an older one. This influences everything about how an individual copes with life, including anxiety and anxiety-related symptoms. Years ago, I created a "Soul Age Spectrum" with ten stages of soul development to assist clients and colleagues in understanding how this influences mental health conditions and coping altogether. The spectrum ranges from infant to ancient souls with descriptions of each respective level. The stages of the spectrum explain the virtues each level represents, the milestone they must reach in order to move to the next level and what their biggest challenges tend to be in getting there. With anxiety in mind, soul age has a direct impact on how an individual views and copes in the world. Taken in consideration with all other human and soul factors, the age of a person's soul can greatly influence both the experience of anxiety and how a person chooses to heal from it.

Astrological Personality

Astrology has existed for several thousand years and goes far beyond the horoscope you may read each day. In ancient times, it was inseparable from astronomy, originating in Mesopotamia and evolving through numerous countries to the many forms that are used today. The field consists of interpreting the influence of the stars and planets to help individuals understand yet another aspect of how they function within the human condition. Personality and a soul's path can be explained through the use of this method quite accurately and precisely, despite the fact that mainstream professionals often dismiss it.

I learned to integrate basic astrology into psychotherapy sessions over two decades ago as I came to understand how directly it impacts a person's personality and their ability to cope. Certain astrological signs and combinations of astrological characteristics are more likely to experience certain symptoms and circumstances just as a result of their profile. In fact, skilled astrologers can predict when an individual might face certain health and mental health crises by looking at an in-depth personal chart. While astrological personality is but one aspect that influences the experience of anxiety, when taken into context with the other human and soul factors, a much richer and fuller picture of an individual's struggles and life journey comes into view.

Planetary Influences

The planets really can align to either make positive things happen or create chaos within a person's life. Related to astrology, planetary alignment often helps to explain why certain mental health concerns are exacerbated or triggered and why these may occur on a cyclical basis. I learned about this from a male psychiatric nurse in my first job within the mental health field. I worked as a psychological technician in both an adolescent and an adult inpatient unit at a hospital near where I completed my undergraduate education. Upon arriving for my evening shift, he noted that it would be a busy and stressful night because a full moon would be rising that evening. I quickly realized that what he said was true, with many of the patients creating atypical chaos throughout the evening. Now, I stay informed about many other celestial events so I know how to both manage my own emotions and guide patients and soul-healing clients through these potentially trying times. Some first responders such as police and other emergency workers as well as various medical professionals (emergency room, psychiatric and obstetric practitioners) often keep track of planetary schedules as well. For those who struggle with anxiety, certain planetary events can create particularly uncomfortable energy, thus triggering symptoms that may have been well managed prior to the event.

I was twenty years old when I started the job mentioned above. However, I've never forgotten that vital knowledge. In fact, I consider it part of my early training to become a holistically based psychologist.

Soul Path/Destiny

Sometimes mental health concerns and/or anxiety-provoking events are embedded in a soul's journey, whether it is to learn lessons for themselves or create circumstances for those around them to learn. You will discover more about this when I discuss the Soul Matrix later in this chapter. The soul's tapestry of life may reflect this as they learn whatever they are supposed to as a result of having anxiety, panic or other anxiety-related responses. It is important to understand that anxiety, as part of a soul path, is simply an artifact of what that person is supposed to experience as part of their human condition. This could be for any number of reasons, the core to be determined by the individual themselves given that everyone has their own set of lessons, experiences and circumstances that makes their human condition their own. Once a person looks at their lives through this wider lens, they can go about their healing process using instances where anxiety is high as cues to dig deeper into understanding what they are supposed to learn and how they can use this information to evolve beyond their concerns.

Karmic Contracts

Karma is more than a punishment for something a person has done wrong. In Hinduism and Buddhism, it is considered the sum of a person's actions in this and previous states of existence. But it is also considered part of destiny or fate. A karmic contract is an agreement the soul makes to experience something, with or without other souls involved, as part of their journey through life. Sometimes karmic contracts create disturbance simply because it is how the soul agreed to either learn certain lessons or create the opportunity to learn for someone else. Karma, in this conceptualization, isn't something that is done *to* us, it is actually something done *for* us for the sake of initiating growth. While a person may not want to experience anxiety, sometimes it is part of their soul path because the innermost part of them agreed to have anxious responses as part of their experience within the human condition. It takes a skilled soul-healing practitioner to help a person determine the karmic cause of anxiety and/or any other mental health concern, but those who become conscious about these concepts can often figure it out on their own.

Soul Injury

I've mentioned soul wounding several times already in this book. While anxiety can certainly be caused by current-life experiences or genetic predisposition within the human condition, it can also result from involvements in past lives. The origin of the discomfort might lie in factors that occurred before the human was even born. As mentioned in section one, various soul wounds can exist, including tragic loss of a loved one, which causes separation anxiety in this lifetime, severe illness that manifests in this lifetime as health anxiety about one or more conditions, fear of certain circumstances, people or animals that is otherwise unexplainable, and more. Remember, the soul can hold energetic imprints of wounds from the current or any prior lifetime. If unresolved, these wounds can become activated regardless of obvious present origins. Once again, an experienced soul-healing specialist may be needed in order to help an individual discover the root of unexplained anxiety in this lifetime.

Past-Life Trauma

Closely related to soul injury, past-life trauma can directly impact the experience of anxiety in the current lifetime.

Claustrophobia, agoraphobia, panic and generalized anxiety can all have past-life origins. Social anxiety can stem from past-life ridicule or public death. Past life regression therapy (PLRT) often unveils traumatic experiences that would otherwise be left unattended. I've had numerous clients tell me they sense tragic pasts when they think of certain circumstances, some saying they have vague memories of something terrible happening but not in this lifetime. Personally, I've experienced spontaneous past-life memories that have explained difficult relationships, a fear of drowning and deep levels of grief. Once uncovered, the emotional discomfort dissipates, likely because *The Three Levels of Healing* (Intellectual—understanding, Emotional—release of feelings, and Soul—energetic imprint) simultaneously occur. When past-life trauma exists but isn't attended, anxiety in this lifetime can persist.

ANCESTRAL SUFFERING

The concept of ancestral suffering has grown in popularity over the last several years. Ancestral healing is considered as the process of revealing and releasing inherited wounds and traumas that have been passed down by our ancestors. In the previous chapter, I discussed epigenetic imprints as a human factor. Here, I emphasize that ancestral healing is a spiritual term used to describe a healing process an individual often undergoes to positively affect not only their own lifetime but the lineage of wounds and trauma ancestors held before them. For instance, when an individual breaks the chain of a long line of abuse or disfunction in a family, this can be considered a release of an ancestral wound. People of certain cultures also heal the lineage in restoring the names of their ancestors to sacred lands, military registers and other historical markers that had previously not been acknowledged. Even more male and female souls are working to heal ancestral injuries through healing gender wounds that have long been present in generations. For example, more males are currently learning to express emotions and many women are working to empower themselves to overcome adversity or discrimination. Often in the process of working with psychotherapy and soul-healing clients, I point out that the work a person is doing to heal from their own wounds is assisting in not only breaking a chain of events but also changing the acceptability of certain historical transgressions as a whole. The Me-Too Movement is just one example. In this way, the client is participating in the evolution of their given gender.

When it comes to anxiety, there are countless events in the existence of humans that could be cause for ancestral healing. As consciousness increases, so does the soul's interest in healing the collective wounds the world carries. Anxiety is but one example of how the human condition can be affected by our ancestral wounds.

Soul Composition

Advanced soul-healing professionals understand the importance of how a soul was created and how that impacts an individual in their human condition. Each soul has been "born" or created with various energetic elements, each different depending on the composition that soul needed as part of their journey from the very beginning of their existence to the end of their soul path. Remember, the soul can be explained by energy—the essence that is at the core of an individual—the life force that exists deep within. Each soul's energy is "compounded" differently, according to many of the factors I've already mentioned and how each conjoins to create the biggest picture of a soul's overall existence, including their experience within the human condition. The composition of a person's soul may influence the experiences he/she has along their soul path, sometimes causing an anxious response as part of their journey. In other words, sometimes it is how the soul itself was created that contributes to whether anxiety exists. While human genes may predispose an individual to anxiety, the "soul DNA" might as well.

Keep in mind, astrological personalities change from lifetime to lifetime. However, soul composition remains the same and may only be activated according to whatever the circumstances and lessons assigned to that lifetime may present.

Starseed History

Starseed origination is yet another concept that only very advanced soul-healing specialists would understand, but is important to mention for those who choose to excavate the origin of anxiety to this level. Just as the geographical location listed in the human factors may impact the experience of anxiety, *where* the soul was created might as well. I realize this is a foreign idea for most readers, but for some who have extensively read spiritual literature it will make some sense. The concept of starseeds is actually not a recent phenomenon conjured up by sci-fi writers. Many ancient civilizations believed in the existence of beings that came from the stars and possessed advanced abilities. The Maya, Inca, Egyptian, Native Americans,

Dogon, Tswalan, Aborigines and most other native cultures believed that star beings (extraterrestrials to some) provided them with the wisdom, knowledge and technology to create their civilizations. While often masked far beneath the experiences and personality of the human condition, sometimes identifying the starseed history helps a spiritually oriented individual more fully understand their challenges within the human condition.

Soul Matrix

The soul matrix refers to the complete "constellation" of factors that a soul holds as part of their own evolutionary path throughout the current and all lifetimes. This includes how their own matrix affects and intersects the matrices of any other soul along their journey. Understanding a soul's matrix illuminates the meta-level integration of the multifaceted nature of the evolutionary existence of that individual. This big picture understanding includes all branches of the human condition depicted in the *Soul Health Model*™, the human factors that affect each branch and all of the soul factors you've read about in this book. It is much like a multi-dimensional mapping of every single aspect of every lifetime a soul has experienced since the moment it came into existence. While the soul matrix may not be necessary to see or understand in order to identify and treat anxiety, advanced practitioners can see how all aspects fit together for an individual in a 3-D way. This level of consciousness is rare but possible and it can lend important insight for those who seek this level of understanding as part of their healing journey.

Soul Mastery/Integration

Soul mastery and integration can be seen as the ultimate, simultaneous alignment of all branches of health with all human and soul factors. Essentially, according to evolutionary and spiritual ascension literature, no human on this planet, including myself, has reached this level. The human condition provides our fodder for growth and we "graduate" from it in order to no longer incarnate. It doesn't mean we cease to exist; it simply means we move onto the next step of our existence. This could mean moving on to a new planetary experience or to another dimension of reality altogether, depending on our soul's destiny and path beyond being human. Needless to say, anxiety (among many other things) would have to be healed in order to reach this level.

The Body, Mind and Soul Picture of Anxiety

As I wrote this book, I shared chapters with colleagues who also do spiritual work with clients but haven't fully conceptualized anxiety as directly rooted in soul-based factors. Nearly all said they didn't realize the field of medicine started with the idea the soul was a strong influence since it is never mentioned in training now, or only in passing if they were mental health practitioners who learned about Carl Jung. Even though many of my colleagues do various forms of energy- or soul-healing work, they hadn't put together the tapestry of strongly connected human and soul factors until they saw the *Whole Soul Model©* and understood the meta-level picture. Even I—someone who does this work all the time, hadn't fully acknowledged the extremely complex nature of how we experience life. It is no wonder understanding and treating anxiety or any other mental health condition is so complex.

Just as I hear "That's the first thing that makes sense" from clients when I explain the soul-based connection of their concerns, my colleagues say the same. Perhaps the fact that *The Whole Soul Model©* put all of the factors into one visual image for the first time was what allowed these professionals to tie them all together as well. Or perhaps the world is just ready for next-level healing. Regardless, my hope is that this information expands your thoughts and opens the door for deeper healing.

As the saying goes, "A picture says a thousand words". In this case, *The Whole Soul Model©* probably says more than that when it comes to healing.

PART THREE

ANXIETY: THE NEW TREATMENT PARADIGM

*We see the world piece by piece, as the sun, the moon,
the animal, the tree; but the whole of which these
are the shining parts, is the soul.*

RALPH WALDO EMERSON

CHAPTER ELEVEN

SOUL-INFORMED CARE: A WHOLE SOUL APPROACH TO UNDERSTANDING ANXIETY

*Let no one persuade you to cure the head until he
has first given you his soul to be cured,
for this is the great error of our day, that physicians
first separate the soul from the body.*

PLATO

Many people undergo years of treatment and understand little of why the warning signs arose in the first place. Around the time I wrote the final chapters for this book, I led one of my favorite one-day retreats, a day designed to help individuals identify a theme for the upcoming year based on what their soul wants them to work on instead of what a person thinks they *should* address from an intellectual level—a common mistake that causes much frustration when goals are unmet. The very first person who introduced herself talked about a long history of social anxiety, lack of confidence and periodic panic reactions. She bravely shared her story and pushed through her discomfort. The woman noted that her anxiety started around age four with no incident of known trauma or other stress-initiating event. Not knowing how she would respond, I cautiously shared what I saw from an intuitive perspective—that her anxiety appeared to stem from past-life issues, particularly some sort of public ridicule. She paused, then told me it was the first thing that made sense given all of the years she's tried to figure out what first initiated her concerns. Nothing else could explain the sudden onset of her anxious symptoms.

I receive this response often when I suggest and explain that soul-based factors are part of the origin of mental health concerns. Anxiety, in particular, seems like it should follow a precipitating event, but often it arises in a way that seems spontaneous, with or without a genetic predisposition to the condition. Keep in mind *The Three Levels of Healing*; when a person connects the dots intellectually, the first step of resolution has taken place.

Several women within the workshop also noted anxiety about readiness to let their children grow into adults, a few saying they hovered over them to the detriment of their development. As mentioned in earlier chapters, separation anxiety—in this case the parent letting go—is often based in loss of a loved one in prior lives. Karmically speaking, it is not uncommon for souls to travel through lifetimes in soul groups—individuals or family members who choose to share relationships in multiple lifetimes for the sake of learning and growth. In the case of separation anxiety, it is common for paired souls to come back together to overcome wounds experienced in previous history. This can cause an over-identification with another soul until the traumatic experience is healed and both souls can go on to live more freely having healed the wounds.

Without understanding soul-based factors that may play a role in current life challenges, full resolution of concerns may not be possible. The remainder of this book will explore an expanded method in assessing and treating anxiety to include the soul aspects of whole soul health.

Soul-Informed Treatment of Anxiety: The New Treatment Paradigm

An integrated traditional and soul-based treatment protocol is likely to be adopted in the years to come as more practitioners and patients come to understand the deeper origin of some anxiety-related disorders. While treatment of the body and mind will continue to be important, soul-based assessment and methods of caring for patients within the healing process are essential for full resolution to occur. Knowing when soul-based factors need attention is the biggest challenge.

The term Trauma-Informed Care (TIC) was first used in 2001 by Harris and Fallot to shift the focus from the initial presentation of problems to the possibility of past experience of trauma that influences how a person reacts to certain events. This was intended to expand the understanding of responses to include all biopsychosocial aspects of reactions. It is important to expand the conceptualization of anxiety to include not only the biopsychosocial aspects, but all human and soul-related factors as well. Only then will we comprehend the complete story of anxiety and other mental health concerns.

SOUL-INFORMED CARE MODEL

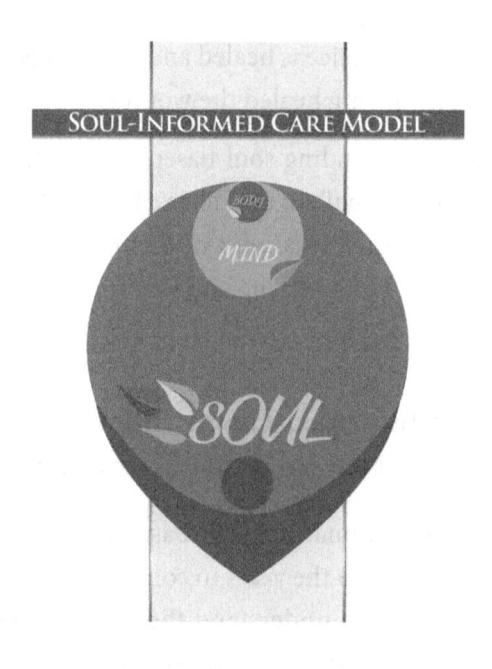

Soul-Informed Care (SIC) is essential in the conceptualization of the treatment of all physical and emotional concerns. While thousands of practitioners have been trained in past-life regression therapy by the internationally esteemed psychiatrist Dr. Brian Weiss and other soul-healing modalities, not all of these professionals are mental health specialists. Unfortunately, very few traditionally trained practitioners interact with soul-healing clinicians, let alone know or understand these techniques, making integrated treatment even more difficult. However, a growing number of mental health professionals are finding value in expanding their understanding of spirituality and soul-based approaches, which adds promise to a potentially groundbreaking field. Psycho-spiritual specialists will someday become an asset to treating all mental health concerns and likely many body-mind-soul-based physical concerns as well. For now, early assessment and awareness of underlying soul-based causes of anxiety is a place to begin.

Assessment of Anxiety Disorders

Body, mind and soul assessment is important to adequately address all aspects of health for those challenged by anxiety disorders. Research is still ongoing for the body and mind treatment of anxiety and many screening tools have been developed to more fully assess concerns. However, as noted in a systematic review of the literature, scientific validation of these tools has been lacking due to inadequate testing procedures. Nevertheless, screening tools are still found to be helpful in providing information regarding patient experience of anxiety.

Body-Based Assessment

Assessment of anxiety disorders usually includes four main components: medical history, current use of prescriptions and over-the-counter (OTC) medications, general symptoms and concerns related to mental health. As part of whole person care, all of these components should still be assessed as part of the "body" aspect of treatment. A healthcare provider generally completes a physical exam and asks about physical symptoms a person may have as part of their anxiety profile. The practitioner usually assesses symptoms to meet criteria based on the Diagnostic and Statistical Manual of Mental Disorders (DSM-5) mentioned in earlier chapters to determine which anxiety disorder is most fitting for reported symptoms. Your medical provider might also use something like the Generalized Anxiety Disorder-7 (GAD-7) inventory to help assess which signs are present. This survey asks seven questions and assesses anxiety based on mild, moderate and severe symptoms. While there are no specific lab tests to identify anxiety, your general practitioner may ask for blood or urine tests to help rule out medical concerns that may produce anxiety-related symptoms. Dietary intake may be assessed to determine whether food or supplements may be contributing to anxious responses.

Note: Specialized genetic testing by trained psychiatric and mental health professionals now exists to help identify genetic markers for anxiety and other mental health concerns, but these are primarily utilized to match psychotropic medications with the correct condition, not to initially identify the concern.

Mind-Based Assessment

Most mental health professionals assess anxiety using a mixture of psychological interviewing and questionnaires that are designed to more closely assess the type of anxiety a person experiences. Practitioners are trained to identify clusters of symptoms that most typically describe particular types of anxiety, then administer various inventories including the GAD-7 and others such as the Beck Anxiety Inventory (BAI), a twenty-one-item questionnaire that generally measures severity of symptoms or the State-Trait Anxiety Inventory (STAI), two questionnaires with twenty items each that measure either state or trait aspects of anxiety. While all have been used for years, the GAD-7 is the most tested for validity. All inventories can offer valuable information to help understand an individual's personal experience with anxiety symptoms.

Further psychological assessment includes exploration of the development of anxiety-related thought processes as well as a general personal history.

With the *Whole Soul Model©*, anxiety can be assessed using the ten branches of the human condition to more fully identify aspects of a person's life that are impacted and/or initiating the experience of anxiety. The twenty human factors (life experiences, trauma, cultural influences, parenting/family or origin dynamics, gender aspects, etc.) should also be thoroughly assessed to understand the individual's symptoms.

In my opinion, the bioenergetic field should be assessed in all individuals who struggle with anxiety reactions. Because many individuals with anxiety tend to be more energetically sensitive than others who do not have anxiety, it is possible that bioenergetic "misfiring" in their overall field, which can cause both immediate and ongoing discomfort, may be the root cause of their reactions. For instance, those who are "empaths"—people who automatically sense the emotions and energetic nature of other individuals—their tendency to absorb and be affected by others' energy often causes anxious responses. These reactions can be quite extreme. While these individuals experience the discomfort themselves, the origin of the energy behind the discomfort often lies outside of that individual. I tell clients who are energetically sensitive that their own energetic field acts much like static cling—other people's energy is attracted to and "sticks" to individuals who empathically absorb the excess energy. This can create a real issue for those who are unaware. Much like a vacuum-effect, empathic individuals attract and hold the energy of those around them. While empaths don't always experience extreme anxiety, many do report feeling overwhelmed while in the presence of others who are anxious.

Regardless, energy-protective strategies exist to help individuals shield the impact of others. Unknown to many traditional practitioners, these strategies are immensely helpful for those who are energetically sensitive, especially those who experience anxiety.

Soul-Based Assessment

In general, few traditionally trained practitioners currently understand soul-based factors when treating mental health concerns, including anxiety. However, many individuals who study spirituality can likely relate many of their concerns to these factors simply by reading this book. While I don't recommend simply assuming that there is something deeper that contributes to unidentified origins of anxiety, for those who are more spiritually or soul aware, you may be able to draw your own conclusions.

As mentioned before, it is not uncommon for me to hear "That's the first thing that makes sense" when working with a client who struggles with atypical anxiety or other unanswered origins of mental health concerns. One client who has long struggled with anxiety sought my services because she knew something deeper was at stake. She had undergone frequent psychotherapy for years and was taking psychotropic medication to manage periodic symptoms. However, nothing eliminated her concerns until we did a regression to find that her anxiety resulted from a number of past lives when she was punished for speaking out.

The woman I mentioned in the beginning of this chapter had experienced public humiliation in a past life, with the residual effects still impacting her through social anxiety today. Many who experience claustrophobia or other atypical manifestations of anxiety can link their current concerns to soul wounds initiated in previous lifetimes. Two clients, who experienced a fear of dogs and birds, respectively, were able to resolve their anxiety-related reactions once past-life trauma was healed.

The best way to identify whether soul-based factors play a part in a person's anxiety is to assess whether current-life origins exist—something the individual can attach to the initial anxious response. If nothing can be identified, it is likely that residual soul-related wounding plays a role in a person's experience of anxiety. When all else fails or if nothing else from a current life can be identified, it is highly possible that past-life trauma or wounding is part of the overall concern.

Our history dates back far before this lifetime. Therefore, nearly everyone on this planet holds some elements of stress from past-life events and circumstances. The more aware of these layers a person can be, the more likely they can address all aspects. As you can see by the diagram here, the body and mind aspects of anxiety are parts of the whole soul's experience, but do not explain the overall picture of a person's experience.

Soul Savvy Exploration of Anxiety-Related Concerns

As mentioned previously, I now train and coach other practitioners, coaches, educators and administrators to understand how soul-based factors affect client/patient health. However, those who read this book likely have at least some interest in spiritual elements. While it takes a trained professional to fully assess the spiritual components of anxiety, there are some questions one can ask to help identify whether any of the sixteen soul-related factors noted in *The Whole Soul Model©* are playing a part in a person's experience of the condition.

Soul Consciousness

- After trying other body/mind methods, do you feel something deeper is at the core of your anxiety?
- By reading this book so far, has something triggered you to seek soul-based care?
- Do one or more of the soul-based factors resonate with you?

Life Lessons

- Has your anxiety helped you learn something about who you are, your circumstances or something else?
- Is there a pattern to your experience of anxiety that might have a bigger meaning?
- Is your anxiety related to overcoming a major milestone as part of your soul's evolution?

LIFE PURPOSE

- Has your anxiety somehow led you to understand your life purpose?

- Is your anxiety keeping you from achieving an intended dream? (Is a life lesson involved?)

- Is your life purpose interfering with or feeding into your experience of anxiety? (Example: Mission to give too much to others if you feel your life-purpose is to help others?)

GENDER HERITAGE

- Do you feel your gender or gender role plays a part in your anxiety?

- Is your anxiety related to your gender heritage? (Past-life wounding due to given genders in past generations? Example: Particular experiences as a male or female?)

- Do you experience gender anxiety related to your personal or professional life?

SOUL AGE

- Certain stages of soul development inherently carry insecurities and stress due to soul maturity. Do you feel this applies to you?

- Certain soul ages can experience persistent confidence and sense-of-self issues. Do these concerns resonate with you?

- If you've never felt like you fit it with those around you because of divergent maturity levels when it comes to looking at life, could soul age influence your experience of anxiety?

Astrological Personality

- Depending on the astrological personality, some combinations of traits can create excessive worry or rumination. Have you explored how your astrological profile might impact your experience of anxiety?

- To a skilled astrologer, sometimes an astral chart can identify personality nuances that impact mental health. Are you aware of any in your chart?

- Also, because our astrological personality inherently provides us with characteristics we are supposed to outgrow in our lifetime, could this be related to how anxiety appears in your life? (Examples, outgrowing a certain characteristic can cause distress.)

Planetary Influences

- Do you notice your anxiety flaring in cyclical patterns? Have you considered whether planetary influences play a part? Some individuals are particularly sensitive to planetary movement and alignment.

- Full moon, Mercury Retrograde, various eclipses and other planetary influences can affect a person's mental health. Have you explored these influences to note patterns in your experience of anxiety? You may want to consider learning more to track any patterns that might exist.

Soul Path/Destiny

- Sometimes a soul chooses to experience certain conditions as part of their soul path/destiny. Usually this is for the sake of learning and/or playing a part in someone else's soul journey as well. In this case, a skilled soul-healing specialist is likely needed to assist in identifying a destiny-based soul factor.

- Do you feel anxiety is part of your life to help you learn certain lessons?

- Has anxiety helped you identify things that need attention in your life?

Karmic Contracts

- Aside from being part of a person's soul path, sometimes karmic agreements have contributed to anxiety in a person's life. It is possible that anxiety has manifested in this lifetime due to something the individual caused for others in a previous one, but in most cases, anxiety arises because it is a cue to become more aware of what you are supposed to learn about yourself as a result of having the anxious responses in general. While karma is not always created as punishment, it is always present as an opportunity to learn and grow.

- Do you feel your anxiety arises when engaged in certain relationships or relationship dynamics? Is there a pattern to your fears? Karmic connections with other souls may activate unresolved issues from past lives.

- Do certain relationships seem more confusing and complicated than they should be? Do they push your buttons? These usually hold karmic significance and will only be resolved when certain lessons or patterns are identified.

Soul Injury

- Many forms of soul injury exist. As mentioned before, a person's energetic field can be damaged from either this lifetime or a previous one. Sometimes that soul brings to a lifetime the energetic wounding that is left over from previous lifetimes. It can come in the form of an energetic program, compassionate connection with another (carrying the anxious energy of another), a vow (to endure anxiety throughout a lifetime), or soul facet injury (carrying various wounds of oneself and sometimes others). Again, it is necessary for an advanced soul-healing specialist to assist in identifying these kinds of soul injury.

- Is the type of anxiety you experience unexplainable given what has happened in your life? If your anxiety can't be linked to something specific in this lifetime, it is likely that it comes from residual wounding from the past that is beckoning to be healed now.

Past-Life Trauma

- Past-life trauma is a significant contributor to current-life anxiety. The energetic imprint left on a soul by trauma can extend between lifetimes and inhibit comfortable function. Have you had glimpses of experiences that can't be linked to those in this lifetime? A trained past-life regression therapist and/or other soul-healing specialist can assist in more fully assessing residual anxiety. Similar to other forms of soul injury, past-life trauma might explain your experience of anxiety now.

- Is there a theme or pattern to your anxiety that doesn't match current-life experiences? Do you have unexplained fears about something?

Ancestral Suffering

- Growing awareness surrounds the idea of ancestral healing. Certain souls have elected to enter the current lifetime carrying the ancestral trauma for all generations that came before them. Asking questions about a person's ancestral heritage may lend insight into whether generational suffering is present.

- Do you have a strong connection with your heritage? Have you observed your elders struggling and have a strong desire to take away their pain?

- Does your experience of anxiety feel heavier or deeper than it should for what you know of others who struggle with anxiety?

Soul Composition

- The composition of a soul—the "ingredients" in which it was created—is sometimes incompatible with the person's current life circumstances or experience on earth in general. There is much discussion among spiritual experts whether the soul's energy can successfully navigate the frequency of energy on this planet. Many theorists suggest that souls such as those who struggle with what would be considered spectrum disorders or neurodivergence are not able to withstand the energies commonly found on this planet. Much will likely need to be explored to further confirm these lines of thought. Some questions to ask:

- Do you feel unusually energetically sensitive to typical earthly events, places, people or circumstances?

- Have you felt like you never fit in with family, friends, your culture or environment? Has this caused anxiety in your life?

- Do you yearn for home, but you don't know what that means?

Starseed History

- For very advanced soul-healing specialists, starseed history may play a part in whether/how a person experiences anxiety in the human condition of clients. Just as people of different nationalities can carry emotional concerns due to traumatic events, it is thought that people whose souls originate from other star systems may also carry "star trauma"—energetic imprints from difficult experiences through their celestial history that has been left unresolved.

- Have you ever felt like you are from another world—not Earth?

- Does your experience of anxiety seem far deeper or less usual than others'?

Soul Matrix

- The Soul Matrix is the "constellation" of factors that affect and impact a person's life, including all of the soul factors listed above. Much like a human's life can seem out of alignment, which causes discomfort, a soul's constellation of factors can feel out of position as well. When one or more soul factors are misaligned, the soul of a human can experience persistent and seemingly unexplainable discomfort. Because our own soul matrix overlaps/intertwines with the matrices of those closest to us, we can experience the stress/distress of others. Understanding the soul's matrix is an advanced skill, but working with someone to assist in the process can be extremely helpful. Seasoned soul-healing professionals are likely the only practitioners who can help you understand, sort and heal a deeply misaligned matrix.

Soul Mastery/Integration

- Mastering the human condition is only part of full healing; mastering and integrating the various aspects or factors of the soul condition are required for complete resolution to occur. Abraham Maslow, an early American Psychologist, studied human needs. At the top of his "needs pyramid" is actualization—the state in which a human masters various challenges of the human condition to appreciate and integrate all needs. Similar to his model, soul mastery/integration describes a point in which a person has evolved beyond both the human and soul factors that inhibit their evolution. Keep in mind, all of us are here to learn and evolve. When we return to live future lifetimes, it is because we haven't fully evolved beyond our challenges or healed what is needed in order to advance. I have found that those who are nearing the completion of their human work often experience far less discomfort related to the human condition. Fewer earthly issues affect them, while still remaining sensitive to the struggles of others. Soul Mastery is not something that necessarily needs attention when assessing and treating anxiety, but it is helpful to understand in the picture of whole soul health.

Humans are complicated beings, which explains why anxiety is also so complicated. Although it might seem overwhelming to learn about all of the factors that may play a part in the experience of distress, not all aspects affect just one individual— each has their own combination or "constellation" of factors that contribute to their discomfort. While the management of anxiety may appear to be a life-long process, getting to the bottom of what caused it can greatly accelerate the healing.

CHAPTER TWELVE

SOUL-BASED MODALITIES TO ASSIST IN THE TREATMENT OF ANXIETY

That which is above is like to that which is below, and that which is below is like to that which is above.
EMERALD TABLET

By now, you understand that anxiety is not always resolvable by treating the body and mind alone. To fully heal, you must include the soul. While the biopsychosocial approach was a good start many decades ago, it is an outdated concept and only addresses three of the ten branches of the human condition and none of the aspects that affect the essence of who a person really is. Much more is at stake when it comes to truly resolving any mental health concern and it is time to take healing to the deepest level.

"As above, so below" is a popular paraphrase of a verse from an early Arabic writing. It first appeared in the late eighth or early ninth century, although no one really knows the original source. While many different interpretations exist, the primary implication is that there is an outer (above) and inner (below) world and neither should be ignored. To date, modern treatment of most conditions—both medical and psychological in nature—have only focused on the body and more recently the mind. To dismiss the deepest inner workings of an individual is no longer enough.

Because very few healing professionals understand the "whole soul" experience, individuals have been left on their own to explore deeper practices that aren't acknowledged or supported in mainstream realms. My hope is that this book will serve to educate both those who struggle with anxiety and the practitioners who treat them. In many cases, it is the patient who introduces nontraditional ideas to the traditionally trained clinician, whether or not these concepts are understood or accepted. It is my belief that the most productive, effective and satisfying treatment occurs when clients/patients and professionals work together for the improvement of overall health. If holistically trained and soul-healing practitioners were added to the mix, much more progress would inevitably be made.

Soul-healing practitioners are trained through all sorts of traditions and modalities. Unfortunately, there is currently no governing body or organization that certifies or licenses a practitioner in many of their chosen traditions. Because modern healthcare typically only approves of modalities which research can support or prove, many very effective treatments are dismissed or are met with disapproval. Hopefully, this will change as the concept of healing expands to include body, mind *and* soul treatment of everyday mental health concerns. Millions of people already seek spiritually based services each year, so it is essential that all aspects of care be acknowledged and embraced as healthcare itself evolves.

Recent studies affirm the need to attend more to the soul. In July of 2023, the Pew Research Group conducted a study related to spiritual and religious beliefs among Americans. The group found that an overwhelming majority of American adults (83%) believe that they have a soul or spirit beyond the physical body. While uncertainty exists about what happens after death, 33% of individuals directly report belief in reincarnation, that number has grown in the last decade. Forty-one percent (41%) of Americans believe in psychics and twenty-nine (29%) use astrology to assist them in daily life. The research also showed that the number of individuals who identify as Christian is steadily dropping, while many who believe in Christianity also report belief in psychics, reincarnation, astrology and other spiritual/non-religious beliefs. While some of these lower statistics might appear to dismiss matters of the soul, the research also made clear that many people simply answered they didn't know what to believe or had no context in which to apply meaning. Regardless of whether a practitioner believes in soul-related concepts, patients are seeking soul-healing services at an increasing rate.

It should be noted that many cultures outside of the United States have long held beliefs about the soul and reincarnation (Hinduism, Buddhism, Jainism, Sikhism, along with some Christian, Islam, Egyptian, Judaist, Greek sects). Basically, every continent had ancient civilizations that led their lives based on the continuity of life. In fact, many famous historical figures believed that the soul traveled through multiple lifetimes: Voltaire (French writer), Henry David Thoreau (American novelist),

Benjamin Franklin (founding father of the United States), Thomas Edison (American inventor), Henry Ford (American industrialist), Carl Jung (Swiss psychiatrist), Walt Whitman (American author/poet), Ralph Waldo Emerson (American essayist), General George S. Patton (American military leader), Charles Dickens (English writer), Giordano Bruno (Italian Dominican friar), Mark Twain (American writer), Edgar Allen Poe (American writer/poet) are just a few. Numerous other world leaders, philosophers, scientists and influencers also openly shared beliefs about how their soul lives on.

With these long-held views, it stands to reason that the "below"—factors of the soul—firmly exist. Now we have to figure out what to do with it given that our innermost self accumulates wounds along the path of both this lifetime and any prior. The remainder of this chapter briefly explores many of the possible soul-based methods that are already present. While many of them might be new to you, several have been practiced for thousands of years. They are presented in no particular order of importance as each soul may require something different in order to heal and evolve.

Methods of Soul-Based Care

In Chapter Six, I wrote about *The Three Levels of Healing*: Intellectual, Emotional and Soul. I emphasized that in the process of healing the body and mind, some soul healing can take place. I also noted that sometimes the first two approaches are not enough to fully resolve issues. If something persists regardless of strongly applied treatment of the body and mind, healing is usually required at a deeper level.

Here, I discuss many methods of treatment that assist in healing the soul. I start with approaches that are more commonly known but likely not directly attributed to soul-based levels of care. Keep in mind; the soul is the essence of who we are. Any healing method that restores our sense-of-self is working in the right direction. However, it isn't until the energetic imprint of a wound on our soul is removed or repaired that we experience full resolution. While many common methods may help a client make progress toward wholeness, soul-based intervention might be necessary to fully finish the process.

A note of caution is warranted as you read ahead. It is important to seek any kind of care for the body, mind and soul only from credible and experienced practitioners. The following chapter will explore how to find soul-healing professionals who can most effectively and professionally assist you on your healing journey.

Inner Child/Self Work

Swiss psychiatrist, Carl Jung, first coined the term "inner child" to explain the child construct or archetype that becomes wounded when stressful or traumatic experiences are encountered at a young age. As mentioned, Jung believed very strongly in the continuous nature of the soul and emphasized the need to heal the young aspects of ourselves that have been wounded. These days, most therapists understand the concept and can assist in the process of healing. However, not all are voiced in the healing of the soul itself. The origin of anxiety often stems from childhood experiences and relief from healing the child within can be greatly beneficial in healing overall.

Emotional Healing/Psychospiritual Counseling

Much psychological care is focused on managing and decreasing the experience of unwanted emotions. When emotional healing techniques are paired with spiritual exploration, healing can often reach deeper regions of our whole soul self. Psychospiritual counseling is based on integrating mind-based interventions with spiritual concepts. However, keep in mind that Christian counseling is different; it often uses scripture and prayer to assist clients on their healing path, but rarely if ever addresses soul-based issues. It is important to keep in mind that many individuals have had negative religious experiences in this lifetime or those prior, so sometimes anxiety stems directly from these events whether directly identifiable or not. Therefore, full exploration of a person's spiritual history may be necessary before engaging in religiously based counseling. In doing a random Internet search, nearly every state now has at least one psychological practitioner who extends their practice to soul-based methods. It is uncertain whether these practitioners have been trained by credible means.

Energetic Healing

Energy healing is now a popular healing system that focuses on restoring the balance and flow of energy throughout the body, mind and soul. Currently, numerous forms of energy treatment exist, all offering techniques to work directly with the physical, emotional and spiritual aspects of well-being. While some practitioners are trained to systematically touch particular energy points or meridians on a person's body, many are trained to work in the person's bioenergetic field to unblock, balance or heal etheric wounds—wounds related to the spiritual world or etheric plane of a person's existence. Clients are fully clothed for energy sessions unless a massage therapist or other body worker integrates energy techniques into their treatment with clients. Energy methods are often used to treat various medical concerns, but mostly focus on mental health. Many bodywork practitioners (massage therapists, estheticians, yoga instructors, etc.) become attuned to their clients' energy and as a result begin to energetically sense what is going on at a deeper level. This often leads practitioners to seek more formal training related to energy techniques.

As mentioned earlier in this book, everything—especially the soul—is energy. In my experience, energy work is immensely helpful for both psychotherapy clients and those who are actively working on healing their soul. Working with a skilled practitioner can be invaluable in the process of healing.

Cord Cutting

Related to energetic healing, "cord cutting" may assist in releasing unwanted/unhealthy connections with other energetic beings (humans, mostly) that might cause anxious reactions or negatively influence your ability to cope. Sometimes we hold energetic ties to those who have been harmful to us in the past. These ties act somewhat like a drain or syphon on our energy. These cords could be related to souls who have been abusive, dominant or controlling and must be released in order to free oneself from the bond once held with that soul. Some energy workers are skilled at assessing these energetic cords and can assist in releasing those energies. Personally, I encourage individuals to work on releasing the cord altogether, not simply cutting the cord. Much like a weed, if an energetic tie is not removed from the "roots", it can resprout and/or spread. As a soul-healing practitioner who is also trained in two different energy healing modalities, I have assisted numerous clients in releasing unwanted energetic cords and other blockages throughout their body and energetic field. All clients experienced liberation from the binds that once held them back.

Somatic Healing

Somatic methods of healing focus on how emotions appear and are stored within the body. Because everything is energy, our body often holds and expresses experiences and emotions, sometimes based in trauma or other unresolved emotional issues. The idea is that this emotional energy is trapped within the body and must be released for healing to occur. Skilled practitioners help clients examine how their physique holds emotion, and explore the meaning behind the emotions and related experiences. They further assist the person in dissolving and processing the emotion as they release it from their energetic storage within the body. Again, while not all somatic practitioners are trained in soul-healing methods, anything that realigns and restores the branches of health (physical, psychological, social, etc.) will inevitably assist in healing the soul as well.

Insight Meditation

Insight meditation is designed to help a person pay attention to and track whatever arises in their body, mind and life as they meditate. Those who are able to tune into their soul are often able to hear what it is saying or requesting as part of their healing and evolutionary process. While the practice isn't specifically designed to teach you to listen to your deepest self, I often teach insight-based methods to listen better and hear the voice of the soul.

Automatic Writing

Besides meditation and other intuitive methods, I both practice and teach automatic writing skills for the purpose of accessing messages from the soul. Automatic writing is a process of producing words on paper, not by conscious intention by the writer but instead, released through subconscious agency. The method includes writing or thinking about a specific question you want answered from a deeper level, then documenting words as they arrive naturally. This approach requires a writer to release conscious thought and open to whatever clarity comes simply as a matter of allowing them to surface. Soul-based writing can be extremely powerful once you master the skill and healing can occur spontaneously as awareness comes to light. Remember, *The Three Levels of Healing* include Intellectual, Emotional and Soul levels; therefore, simply allowing issues to surface that need attention from a soul-based level can accelerate healing.

Shadow Work

Shadow work refers to the process of working with your unconscious mind to uncover the aspects of yourself that you repress and hide from awareness. We all have hidden parts of ourselves we'd rather not see. These darker or damaged parts of us remain obscured but often influence our daily lives whether or not we are aware. Once again, the psychoanalyst Carl Jung first developed the concept of "shadow self" along with the idea of the "persona" we wish to present to others. Because Jung emphasized the need to heal the inner and less conscious self, the process of addressing the shadow side of ourselves inevitably assists in healing the soul. Not all therapists direct attention to this aspect of self, but any form of soul-based healing heals the darker shadows within.

Shamanic Healing

Shamanic practices are based in a system of religious or spiritual practice most associated with indigenous and tribal societies where shamans hold a connection to the otherworld and can assist in healing the sick, communicate with spirits and escort souls of the dead to the afterlife. Shamanic healing has become quite popular and various methods of healing are focused on the soul—releasing unwanted energies, retrieving aspects of self that are fragmented or held by others, releasing ancestral wounds, understanding a soul's journey and more. While their tribes or communities choose true shamans, many modern practitioners are trained in shamanic practices and can call themselves shamanic practitioners. For those interested in indigenous practices, shamanic healing can be quite helpful in healing additional layers of anxiety and other mental health concerns.

Karmic Release

Karma, the energy held between two energetic beings, places or circumstances can hold us back. This karma can be experienced through energetic cords or the energetic "charge" or connection shared with others. Often anxiety exists because of karmic energy created from some sort of lesson that has not been learned. In some cases, souls can be laced with karmic energy because of a "karmic debt" that is owed to another—a situation in which souls are supposed to interact to create the circumstances for one or both to overcome a challenge and/or heal from something in the past. Often the very act of understanding why something happens (the First Level of Healing) is enough to release karmic bonds; however, sometimes more active forms of release are required for resolution to occur. Because everything is energy, the energetic tie or bond we hold with people, places and circumstances can cause emotional disturbance in the form of anxiety, depression or other mental concern. Often, work with skilled practitioners is necessary to dissolve karmic bonds.

Soul Retrieval

Sometimes aspects of ourselves can become fractured or fragmented, particularly when trauma has occurred at the hands of another soul. When particularly karmic ties exist between two human beings, often one energetically holds the other "hostage", maintaining an emotional hold in one way or another. This karmic imprisonment can seriously inhibit and disrupt a person's mental health and ability to move forward. While most soul retrievals are done by shamanic practitioners and certain soul-healing practitioners, sometimes individuals can retrieve aspects of themselves through inner child or shadow work, cord cutting, somatic healing and past life regression. It is not unusual that karmic fragments or facets are energetically held by abusers or other souls who created deep harm. When you think about whole soul health, missing even one small fragment of oneself could create an experience of anxiety. Seeking assistance in identifying missing parts can be extremely helpful in achieving whole person health.

Vision Quests

A vision quest is usually intended as a rite of passage for native cultures as they transition from one developmental milestone to another. The quest encourages and supports the awakening of the individual to their own indigenous wisdom and helps them align with their own divine nature. Quests are performed in many ways, most involving time spent in deep introspection with or without a guide. The intention is to gain a vision of a future self so a soul knows what it is supposed to work on or strive for from that point on. While most vision quests are future-oriented, some involve experiences in which the soul must go back in their history—either this lifetime or prior—to identify aspects of themselves that must be retrieved or collected in order to evolve or move forward. Sometimes vision quests are paired with the use of spiritually identified substances (tobacco, peyote, ayahuasca or other plant-based drugs) but most are intended to organically connect the external spiritual world with the individual's soul. While vision quests can actually provoke anxiety in some people, others seek such experiences to attempt to overcome fears. Caution should be exercised in deciding whether or not a vision quest is right for you.

Ancestral Healing

Ancestral healing is a type of energy healing based on the belief that the actions and experiences of ancestors create a kind of energetic imprint on a person's soul and experience of everyday human life that detracts from happiness, ability to feel joy and move beyond certain dynamics that are passed from one generation to the next. It is a process of using spiritually based rituals to empower individuals in connecting with, repairing and nurturing relationships with ancestors. Usually, the individual experiences some sort of disturbance of trauma that leads them to identify with the pain of their ancestors or generations past. One example includes anxiety and fear that accompanies abuse. Because those who are abused often abuse others, there is often a chain of generations that exhibit abusive behavior. Those individuals who have experienced mistreatment but have been able to break the chain in their family line often must undergo treatment to heal. In the process of healing their own trauma, often they break the chains of neglect and create healthier dynamics for their children who come after them. Sometimes individuals are aware of a strong connection with their elders as they experience healing. The experience of anxiety can have strong ties to past generations and once a person realizes they can heal, they feel empowered to release anxious energy. Ancestral healing has been a common part of indigenous practices and is just recently becoming a more recognized concern and need in modern healing.

Psychedelic Journeying

As mentioned in Chapter Four, psychedelic interventions are rising in popularity as part of treating the body aspects of anxiety. While these methods are designed to create new neural pathways and minimize or eliminate anxious thoughts, they are not directly intended to heal the soul. However, many individuals seek psychedelic journeying from holistic or spiritual practitioners to manage and heal anxiety and other emotional concerns from a soul level of healing. While I am a strong advocate for soul-based healing, I strongly discourage people from seeking this type of treatment if not led by a mental health practitioner. When any form of drug is involved, there is much room for error when highly trained professionals are not involved. I've seen more than one bad outcome, and one is more than enough to convince me that this approach to soul-based healing should be considered only with extreme caution.

Past Life Regression Therapy

In a previous chapter, I mentioned Dr. Brian Weiss, the world-renowned psychiatrist who became a past-life expert. While doing hypnosis with patients to help them manage various mental health conditions, he realized that many patients spontaneously regressed to past lives. He checked the facts and was astounded that patient symptoms often resolved after they revisited and processed their past-life experiences. When it comes to anxiety, patients often experience at least some healing simply by recognizing that their unexplainable symptoms originated through past-life events. Undergoing past-life regression therapy when something is more directly connected to previous trauma can be extremely useful in the process of whole soul care.

Past-life regression therapy (PLRT) involves a form of hypnosis specifically intended to assist a patient in identifying past-life events that caused their concerns. Relatively few therapists are trained in this method of healing and sadly, the majority of those who have been trained in past-life regression are not psychologically trained practitioners. Note that PLRT differs from past-life regression in that the former takes those trained through the actual healing path. Many people who are trained in past-life regression only provide the service because people ask, with no intention of following up for therapeutic reasons. For clients who wish to address anxiety or any other mental health concern through the method of past-life therapeutic treatment, I highly recommend finding a mental health practitioner who is specifically trained to help people through this form of regression.

Astrological Counseling and Assessment

Astrology has existed for thousands of years, but within psychotherapy has been vastly underutilized. Each soul has an "astrological personality" for that lifetime designed to create the emotional experiences that challenge and assist them on their evolutionary journey. We do not incarnate with the same astrological profile every time we enter a new life. Instead, it changes according to which aspects of ourselves we've mastered in previous lifetimes as well as what we are supposed to learn and accomplish in the current life. Seeking astrological counseling can assist a person in understanding not only how their personality affects their everyday experience of human existence (natal chart) but what is likely to transpire in the months and years ahead (progressive chart). There are several different forms of astrology, but skilled astrologers will be able to help you understand how anxiety or anxiety-provoking events may season your life. Astrology can also assist in explaining certain life lessons, life purpose, relationship issues and even potential health concerns (mental health included). Few mental health professionals and even fewer medical practitioners utilize this very useful tool, but those who do can more deeply guide you through your healing journey.

Akashic Readings and Other Intuitive Counseling

The Akashic Records are considered the etheric or energetic records of all things past, present and future, knowing that free will highly influences what happens as an individual moves forward. The record includes all universal events, thoughts, words, emotions and intent in all entities and life forms, not just human. Someone who is trained to read the Akashic Records can energetically tune into a particular soul's story to extract information that would assist in their healing or evolutionary journey. Because anxiety can include origins in this or a past lifetime, a skilled practitioner can assist an individual in identifying how it started and often how to heal it. Intuitive counseling is much the same and can be paired with many other modalities including Tarot Card readings, Chakra readings and far more. Often Akashic and other intuitive readings include information about past lives, karmic "mapping" (identification of a soul's life path including how it is related/intertwined with other souls), exploration of a soul's karmic matrix (the inclusion of all human and soul factors that impact an individual) and various other aspects of life that may affect a person's healing. I have provided Akashic/Intuitive readings for many years and have witnessed instantaneous healing from various emotions that impact mental health.

I always note that intuitive counseling should not be seen as a replacement for mental health treatment, only an adjunct to care despite its usefulness and power. I also note that very few mental health practitioners provide intuitive care in addition to psychotherapy services, so individuals might need to seek this soul-level care beyond what traditional treatment teams can provide. While it is helpful to find professionals who do both, it is possible to locate spiritual experts who can assist you in healing. In the future, I hope to assist more practitioners in learning to integrate these skills.

Soul Realignment

Soul Realignment is a more comprehensive approach than Akashic readings in the provision of soul-based care. It involves helping a person identify how their soul was created (soul composition), where it was created (Starseed history) and any soul-based wounds that might impact a person's day-to-day human life. Sessions are far more extensive than general intuitive or Akashic readings and provide a nice foundation for soul-based healing. I have provided these services for many years as well. For those who seek a deep understanding of soul-based factors that affect everyday life, this method of healing is invaluable.

Soul Coaching

The last few decades have presented an explosion of life- and spiritually-oriented coaches. These professionals may or may not be certified as coaches through national organizations. Some hold therapy degrees, but many do not. Coaching can provide an enormous benefit for people to better navigate life, but few are trained in either formal psychological strategies or in methods to more fully understand the soul. However, as individuals learn to balance their lives and change habits, patterns and mindsets, they often feel relief. When it comes to most forms of anxiety, it is important to seek care from those credentialed to offer it. The same is true for soul-based healing.

As you can see, many soul-healing methods already exist. There are others not discussed here, but the purpose of giving this brief explanation is to expand your awareness of soul-based care strategies that might be available to you. In the next chapter you will learn more about how to decide if these methods are right for you and also how to seek credible services.

CHAPTER THIRTEEN

SEEKING WHOLE SOUL TREATMENT OF ANXIETY

When body, mind and soul are healthy and harmonious, you will bring health and harmony to the world—not by withdrawing from the world, but by being a healthy, living organ of the body of humanity.

B.K.S. IYENGAR

Just a few days prior to writing this chapter, I provided a soul-healing session to a forty-one-year-old woman who contacted me to explore both career/life purpose issues and the karmic relationship with her family of origin. She is from Romania but currently lives in France. When scheduling this session, the client noted she had been engaged in psychotherapy for many years and was well on her healing path. In the last twelve months, she had begun a spiritual journey and realized something deeper was going on. She wanted assistance in discovering what this was.

When I do soul-healing work, I tune into what I call the energetic signature of a person's soul—the essence of that person that is embedded in the sound of their voice. This allows me to uncover the unconscious elements that are at play in their human life. Because everything is energy, I am able to access the deeper levels of an individual's experience through a particular level of meditation so I can explain what is happening at the soul level.

A few days before the session, I received an email message stating the client had had some fleeting memories of abuse as a young child, but these memories didn't align with her current life from what she could recall. She felt these memories might explain emotions—mostly anxiety and depression—that persisted regardless of the intense psychological treatment she had undergone.

During the session I helped her understand that memories of various forms of trauma from past lives were getting confused with this lifetime's events. I explained that the memories were starting to break through as she healed the wounds from this lifetime. I also shared other information that was presented during my meditation that helped to illuminate the relationship with her current family. The distress, anxiety and depression she had experienced all of her life were linked to both karmic energy between she and family members that needed to be resolved in this lifetime and to ancestral trauma her soul had chosen to dissolve as she healed her own wounds. Although the information was a lot to take in, the client was visibly relieved to put the deeper pieces of the puzzle together. Because her current therapist didn't understand soul-level healing, she sought my assistance in addressing this aspect of her whole person care.

This story illustrates the importance of integrating soul-based care into traditional practices. Without knowing to add a soul-healing specialist to the mix, her treatment would have hit a wall and further progress would not be made. As you recall, the First Level of Healing is Intellectual Understanding— the process of connecting dots from one event to the next to make sense of what has occurred in creating discomfort. In helping this client to connect events of her past lives with this one, she can now go on to heal from any remaining body- and/or mind-related concerns that to this point have been left unresolved.

Revisiting The Whole Soul Model and Three Levels of Healing

By now, you realize that many more factors go into treating anxiety and any other mental health concern than previously acknowledged. Whole soul health goes far beyond the factors of the human condition and healing strategies must reach the core origin of a concern to resolve issues completely. It is certain that only body, mind *AND* soul treatment will assist individuals to feel complete and whole again. While current treatment targets the body and mind, they are the smallest aspects of Soul-Informed Care (SIC).

The challenge is that most traditionally trained practitioners and researchers don't know where to start—they completely ignore the soul in the process of providing care to others. My hope is that in the years to come many more professionals will come to understand the essential nature of integrating the biggest influence on overall health—the soul. Only then will we get to the bottom of all physical- and mental health-related concerns.

Whole soul care requires attention to all aspects of health—body, mind and soul. *The Whole Soul Model©* illustrates the complexity of our concerns and provides an essential roadmap to identifying the factors that must be resolved at both the human and soul levels for full resolution to occur, not just the

THE HUMAN CONDITION

THE SOUL CONDITION

treatment of commonly-known symptoms. It is true that attending to these factors takes time, thorough attention and knowing whom to enlist in your whole health care team. However, once resolved, the soul is restored and little disturbance will occur neither in the remainder of a given lifetime nor in those to come.

In integrating whole soul care into treatment of anxiety *The Three Levels of Healing* inherently come into play. We must 1) intellectually understand how our anxiety first occurred, 2) go about releasing and resolving the stored emotional energy related to original events and 3) explore any soul-based factors that may play a part in the current disturbance.

While many wouldn't consider physical health issues to be related to soul-based concerns, often they are. When it comes to health anxiety, it frequently originates from distress experienced in previous lives when a soul had become sick or injured, causing intense emotional discomfort related to chronic health concerns, inadequate treatment at the time, intense suffering and/or residual karmic energy that must be healing in this lifetime. In any case, the experience of anxiety is simply the cue that something needs attention, but until a person explores the soul-based levels—the energetic imprint left of their soul from past wounds—the anxious reactions remain. Until individuals and practitioners expand their perspective to include soul-based healing, treatment will only get so far.

Whole Soul Treatment/Care Plan

There are several things to consider when integrating Soul-Informed Care (SIC) into the treatment of anxiety. These include when to seek care beyond what is offered to treat the body and mind, how to learn more about available options, how to determine which modalities might help the most, how to find well-trained and credible professionals, how to know whether you are ready for soul-based methods, understanding the power and limitations of soul-healing and also any contraindications for attempting soul-based approaches when also undergoing other more traditional forms of treatment. Each will be explored here.

WHEN TO SEEK SOUL-BASED CARE

Although treatment of anxiety should always include attention to the body, mind and soul, knowing when to seek soul-based care is important to consider. In many cases, physical symptoms are the first to get someone's attention enough to acknowledge something is out of alignment even though the misalignment may have been in place for quite some time. In other cases, anxiety seems to come out of the blue, with no direct link to an event or clear constellation of concerns. Both forms can indicate soul-based factors, but stem from different types or combinations of deeper unresolved worries. Either way, because anxiety causes disturbance in everyday life, the body, mind and soul are all at play and all should be taken into consideration.

Most people seek what is already known; those who struggle with anxiety typically only know to seek body and mind care and are often inherently suspicious of these approaches. If a person is aware of spiritual concepts, they may already know that soul-based factors may exist. These individuals may seek immediate attention through practitioners who can assist them. However, those who are new to the concept of soul-based care may need time to consider 1) whether they have fully addressed anxiety from a body and mind perspective, 2) whether these methods have provided acceptable management of concerns and 3) whether they feel comfortable seeking assistance from a soul-healing practitioner to help them in fully resolving the origin of the concern.

The rule of thumb is this: if body and mind treatment methods have not resolved anxiety-related responses, there is likely something deeper going on and only soul-based methods will help to fully resolve concerns. The decision to seek soul-based healing then lies with the person. However, if a practitioner is aware of the possibility of deeper concerns, they may recommend further exploration with someone who specializes in dealing with these matters. Much like any physical or mental health concern, both a patient/client and a practitioner should work together to create options that will resolve anxiety. As Soul-Informed Care (SIC) becomes more known and additional practitioners understand the importance of treating deeper issues, further options for care will develop.

How to Learn About Available Options

While I specialize in soul-based healing, I'm also the first person to encourage discernment when learning about options that are available to help you heal. While many holistic and spiritually based practitioners exist, not all understand the intricacies of mind/body/soul care. I intend to change that as I train practitioners, coaches, educators and administrators to integrate whole soul care into their practices; however, until then, learning about possible options is up to the person who chooses to seek such services.

This book provides a broad perspective on modalities and methods that can provide great assistance in healing the deeper origins of anxiety. However, a person seeking care should know that many who provide these options are not medical or psychological professionals, so you may need to be the person at the hub of your own treatment team. Also, because many traditionally trained practitioners lack the understanding about soul-healing practices, you may be on your own to learn about options.

While a few medical professionals have been trailblazers in soul-based care, such as psychiatrist, Brian Weiss who greatly expanded knowledge about past-life regression therapy, many soul-healing strategies are still lesser known. Perusing the Internet will provide some viable information, but one must practice discernment for information and sites that appear to hold integrity. Many books and YouTube videos exist regarding various approaches, but again, thorough exploration of credible information is essential in deciding upon care.

As part of training other practitioners to understand whole soul care, I'm creating an international directory of practitioners who are reputable in their given fields. Unfortunately, many soul-based professionals are still hesitant to openly admit they provide these services. I hope more practitioners choose to enhance their practices as body, mind and soul treatment is more widely known, accepted and embraced.

How to Determine Which Soul-Based Modalities Might Help

As a soul-healing specialist, I'm biased that the soul must be addressed in any concern, whether experienced through the body or mind. I believe very strongly in treating the whole person, not just the symptoms a client experiences. My mode of care always takes into consideration how the soul influences all aspects of discomfort related to a person's experience of the human condition. While the body and mind are first-line focal points for the modern treatment of anxiety, to me, they still represent the smallest aspect of an individual. As Hippocrates, the founding father of medicine, stated, the soul is present in every illness and should not be dismissed. The bottom line is that soul-based modalities will always provide further information to help heal anxiety and other mental health concerns. The question for whether or not to seek care has more to do with readiness, comfort and the availability of options.

How to Find Well-Trained and Credible Professionals

Soul-Based approaches to care are typically not currently provided by practitioners who are part of a traditional or conventional healthcare system. There are several reasons for this. First, science has eliminated spiritual and soul-based care over the centuries because it is impossible to identify where the soul resides and/or explain how it operates to influence the body and mind. Although some medical professionals have become advocates for endorsing the importance of the soul (Dr. Larry Dossey—pharmacy and internal medicine, Dr. Eben Alexander—neurosurgeon, Dr. Deepak Chopra—internal medicine, Dr. C. Norman Shealey—neurosurgeon, and more), it still has not made its way into modern medicine.

Admittedly, it will take some digging to find credible representatives of soul-based healing. I always recommend reading as much as you can through books and other reputable resources to understand how to recognize whether a professional is credible and skilled. Interestingly, I have found very good practitioners on both sides of the fence—those who are highly educated in many different fields and modalities (because they are on their own healing or spiritual journey so they come from both personal and professional experience) and those who may not hold a high educational degree but who inherently understand the essence of the soul. These individuals are often able to help a person either access their own inner wisdom or can energetically read what is going on from a deeper level (whether they do energy work, are intuitive counselors or shamanic/other healing practitioners).

Because I hold a Ph.D. in Counseling Psychology, two master's degrees (Agency and Community Counseling and Public Health), completed a post-doctoral fellowship in Family and Community Medicine, served as medical school faculty and have received training in multiple traditional and holistic methods of healing, people find me credible without much thought. However, this will not always be the case when you seek services.

The World Wide Web has allowed greater access to individuals who may be able to assist in soul-based methods, even if they practice from far away. Not all services need to be rendered in person, particularly intuitive and/or Akashic readings, past-life readings/regression, soul realignment, some shamanic practices and even some energy-based healing techniques. Remember, because everything is simply a different form of energy, skilled practitioners can often assist you from across the globe. If you know of someone who has already accessed care from a soul-healing professional, their word of mouth may be the best evidence of credible care.

My Soul Health Scholars Certifications (*Level One*—Soul Health Scholar, *Level Two*—Advanced Soul Health Scholar, *Level Three*—Master Level Soul Health Scholar and *Level Four*—Sage Level Soul Health Scholar) are intended to help individuals and practitioners find credibly trained professionals who can understand whole soul health and provide soul-healing services. Until more people are trained in systematic methods of understanding whole soul care, it is up to the individual to research whether practitioners can offer what is needed.

I tell people it is hard enough to find someone who cuts your hair the way you'd like, so take the time to find someone whose approach fits your needs.

How to Know if You Are Ready for Soul-Based Methods of Treatment

People don't change or seek care unless they are tired enough of themselves or their situations. When considering treatment for anxiety, once you've exhausted options for care that bring sustainable relief, it may be time to consider what else may help to resolve your concerns.

Spiritually minded individuals already tend to look for options that exist to treat deeper origins of concerns or to at least apply meaning to what they experience. Because the First Level of Healing—Intellectual Understanding—helps to provide meaning for how an individual's anxiety first began, seeking information about soul-based factors can lead to greater resolution of concerns. Whether or not further soul-based treatment is necessary will depend on the individual's particular circumstances and needs.

In many cases, soul-healing clients seek my services because they know something deeper is influencing their discomfort beyond what traditional methods have provided. Because I integrate soul-based care into a traditional understanding of concerns, both psychotherapy and soul-healing clients are generally motivated to get to the bottom of their concerns. I know this integration is unique, but it greatly informs what I do. Training others to understand deeper levels of concern will inevitably help more individuals to receive body, mind and soul treatment in the years to come.

Understanding the Power and Limits of Soul-Based Care

Soul-based care is an immensely powerful approach to healing anxiety and other mental health concerns. Not only can it help to identify the true origin of a disorder, it can also provide a person with the opportunity to heal just by acknowledging the depth of the wound. This book provides a brief explanation of many types of soul-based healing. Many more exist. However, the more you read about and experience this level of care, the more you will heal all aspects of who you are—body, mind *and* soul. It is not uncommon that a person experiences unexpected physical relief (body-level) even when the healing strategy is focused on soul-level intervention. Thoughts and reactions that once plagued the mind are often also resolved. While extensive attention to the body and mind are the common focus of traditional care, often it isn't until the soul is healed that true resolution occurs.

That said, there are limitations to soul-based care as well. I don't want people to assume just by seeking soul-based care that all of their concerns will vanish. Keep in mind that our soul has accumulated wounds throughout many lifetimes, including the current one. This means that sometimes resolving these concerns will take some time.

Also, keep in mind that particular soul factors infer that the experience of anxiety and other mental health concerns are linked to lessons which must be addressed for a soul to evolve in the current lifetime. Certainly, once learned, a person's symptoms will resolve. But sometimes the lessons run deep so that individual doesn't forget to grow. Also, soul age—the age of a person's soul—cannot be accelerated; the individual "graduates" to the next level as they reach the next milestone along the way. Sometimes the discomfort of anxiety exists as part of how that person is supposed to outgrow certain thoughts and behaviors. While many of the soul-based factors need to be healed to dissolve the energetic imprint left on a person's soul, others may persist simply because they catalyze growth in the direction of a person's necessary soul path. It's complicated, but so is the human condition. And the whole soul experience is definitely complex, as you now see. Regardless, integrating soul-based care into the treatment of anxiety can lend valuable information that allows a person to understand themselves better, which adds to their intellectual level of healing.

Contraindications for Integrating Soul-Based Methods with Body and Mind-Based Care

I would be remiss to not mention possible contraindications of integrating soul-based methods into care. While I may be biased that the soul is part of any and all forms of misalignment in health, whether physically or mentally based, soul-based care is not for everyone.

I noted earlier in this book that souls can become fractured or fragmented at a deep level to the point of triggering intense reactions. People with extreme anxiety are cautioned when considering soul-based care in the three following scenarios.

One: If anxiety reactions are not already reasonably managed, soul-based care could disrupt the process of teaching a person how to observe their symptoms, attend to emotional triggers and intervene when discomfort becomes extreme. Treating the body and mind are still essential components to whole soul care. Soul-level healing is more effective once physical and emotional symptoms are identified and applied.

Two: If an individual wants to bypass body- and mind-based care, assuming only the soul is involved, soul-based care is not recommended. This book is about treating all aspects of an individual's experience of anxiety and emphasizes whole soul care. While the soul might be at the base of how a person's anxiety originated, failing to attend to the human aspects—the body and mind—can leave a person in distress.

Three: If an individual is actively psychotic, currently hospitalized for psychiatric concerns or has lost their sense of current reality, soul-based methods are not recommended. Whole soul care includes attention to both the human condition and the soul condition. If the human condition is not aligned to the point of managing daily life, this must be attended to first in order to ensure that soul-based factors are accessible in a healthy and clear way. Although psychiatric disruption may actually be an indicator of soul-based wounds, individuals must first address the human factors that will prepare them for soul-based care once ready.

Even as a psychological professional with decades of experience, I decline doing soul-healing strategies for anyone in the above situations. While, to me, the soul's influence is apparent in every thought, feeling and behavior, we are still here to live the current life and must attend to our immediate human condition to effectively and safely treat the soul. Once an individual experiences some relief within the human condition, they are far more ready to understand and address matters of the soul.

Like any other physical or mental health concern, it is important to explore all aspects of anxiety-related care, including both viability and availability of treatment methods. When it comes to healing anxiety, the most diagnosed disorder around the world, soul-based care can add both an integral layer of understanding of the origins of the condition and offer many less-known tools to minimize the often life-diminishing impact. Soul-based care can possibly heal a person altogether.

Body, mind *and* soul-based care offer the opportunity to completely resolve this widespread condition.

CHAPTER FOURTEEN

INTEGRATIVE CARE: BODY, MIND AND SOUL TREATMENT OF ANXIETY

You are the sum total of the body, mind and soul, and each of these aspects of you has a purpose and a function, but only one has an agenda: the Soul.
NEALE DONALD WALSCH

Many years ago, I contracted with a national company to provide continuing education workshops for healthcare providers across the country. I traveled to various regions to teach about integrating spirituality into practices and used my *Soul Health Model*™ to illustrate the many facets of the human condition that needed simultaneous attention when treating patients. I used the terms "integrative health" or "integrative psychotherapy" in some of the titles or descriptions for the topics I taught. The company printed and mailed all materials to the designated sites ahead of my arrival. Early on, I realized that they had mistakenly changed the wording to read "integrated", which was a catch term used at the time to describe how behavioral health practitioners were being added to medical practices to offer care at the same office. I used this as a teaching example of how the words are actually quite different.

"Integrated" refers to the addition of practitioners to a practice, but does not necessarily mean that the practitioner practices "integrative" care—the term used to emphasize the use of multimodal interventions and complementary health approaches to provide whole person care. Care of this sort is generally assumed to be provided by one person, not a team working in one building or health system. The words might imply a subtle difference, but holistic practitioners are trained to think quite differently from those educated in traditional methods, conceptualizing and treating individuals from all aspects of their being as they address needs. These days, even general practitioners don't practice whole person care because they are expected to refer patients out for all specialty concerns. I remember general practitioners completed simple mole removals, gynecological exams, nutrition education and more. Now they barely touch you during annual physicals and refer out for anything that isn't involved in basic provision of care. Very little is either integrated or integrative in modern healthcare these days, leaving no room for attention to the soul. Unfortunately, that often leaves whole person care to the individual, not their provider.

Future of Treatment for Anxiety and Other Mental Health Concerns

Millions of people already seek soul-healing services each year, many of whom struggle with anxiety and other mental health concerns. The constant quest to determine the core of unexplained issues may end when the soul is considered as part of everyday treatment. That time in which the soul is fully integrated into traditional care is a long way away, but those who read this book will have a head start on understanding the entirety of what body, mind and soul medicine is really all about. Integrating the soul into treatment doesn't mean something new is on the horizon; it means that the world has finally come full circle back to what the founding fathers of medicine and, subsequently, psychology felt treatment should include all along.

The future of treatment for all concerns, whether physical or emotional in nature, deserves the opportunity to integrate the soul into care. In fact, your soul deserves to have the attention it needs in healing. While most treatment is focused on the body first, it is the smallest component of the big picture. It is true that the biological aspects of healing must be addressed as part of treating anxiety, but only a few human factors contribute: genetics and biochemistry, bioenergetic field, related illness and possibly stage of life. All other aspects that contribute to the experience of anxiety have nothing at all to do with the physical aspect of the human condition. Significantly more aspects related to the mind—the psychological aspect of life (psychosocial factors) exist, but still much more falls outside of this realm.

Someday, the world will go back to recognizing the essence of who we are as the most important aspect of healing. In the meantime, I hope to provide ongoing tools and information to empower you to seek soul-healing services on your own.

Reconceptualization of Anxiety Disorders

Traditional practitioners and scientists have worked very hard to uncover the source of anxiety-related concerns and to develop methods to treat them. It is human nature to work with what we know, but it is also our nature to evolve—that is why we exist. Although the medical model quickly lost touch with the soul, it is time to bring it back to its rightful place in whole person care.

The Soul Health Model™ expands the understanding of anxiety to include the ten key branches of the human condition that impact or influence everyday life. As explored in previous chapters, each branch explains layers of how anxiety may have formed for an individual in the current lifetime. However, it isn't until whole health is conceptualized from the soul level that the full picture is considered. The expanded model—The Whole Soul Model© helps to detect additional human factors that may influence the experience of anxiety. Without attending to factors such as cultural influences, gender aspects, generational

THE WHOLE SOUL MODEL - TREE

THE HUMAN CONDITION

mindset, epigenetic imprint, constructs/social programming, core motivations and more, even the human side of anxiety may not be fully addressed.

Finally, the "roots" of the expanded model deserve the utmost attention when addressing the source of anxiety-related conditions. The roots sustain a tree, but also influence its overall health as well. Much is currently being learned about the actual roots of trees and research has found that these foundational aspects play a key role in not only how the individual tree functions, but also how it interacts with others to sustain life.

THE WHOLE SOUL MODEL - ROOTS

THE SOUL CONDITION

Like the roots of an actual tree, the roots—the unseen soul factors of the individual—must gain attention if an individual is to fully thrive within the conditions it is placed. In this case, it is the human condition that suffers if the soul is dismissed or left unattended. Just as trees cannot live without roots, a human will not feel whole unless all aspects of them are acknowledged and taken into consideration through a healing process.

If the soul was considered, reconceptualization of anxiety and all other mental health disorders would change the path of treatment drastically. Not only would the course of action expand to include soul-healing strategies, the necessary duration of treatment would likely shrink in many, if not all cases. Once you get to the true core of what causes any illness, treatment protocols are streamlined to directly address what is misaligned. The soul is no different. Once soul-based factors are identified and addressed, the way in which anxiety is managed and possibly cured will completely change. I hope to see this happen during my lifetime.

Creating a Treatment Team

While it is unlikely that traditional medicine will change to include the soul in the treatment of conditions of the body and mind anytime soon, the interest is obviously growing. Nearly every day I receive email messages or phone calls from healthcare practitioners who have somehow come across my work and want to know more. Almost daily, I also receive inquiries about soul-healing services from clients—many saying they are healthcare providers, themselves. Although the soul is not mainstream yet, I'm hopeful that more practitioners will understand the importance of bringing it back to life.

Socrates, a philosopher who lived in the time medicine was born, said, *"The law presumably says that it is finest to keep quiet about the soul, and not to meddle with it, but to let it go and to take care of everything else. And therefore if the head and the body are to be well, you must begin by curing the soul; that is the first and essential thing."* In an ideal world, soul-healing practitioners would already be integrated into care for anxiety and other mental health disorders. Until then, it is up to most patients to coordinate care that includes the body, mind *and* soul.

It is encouraged that those who struggle with anxiety explore options for soul-based treatment according to what they think may assist in their healing. Hopefully, by reading this book, you have resonated with certain soul factors that may influence your experience of anxiety-related conditions. This will assist in determining what type of healing strategies to include in your path to whole health. If not, certain soul-healing practitioners may know how to help you explore this further. While most traditional practitioners don't currently have an understanding of soul-based strategies, it might be you who influences them the most; it may be the patient who educates their medical and psychological caregivers to learn more.

When possible, search for terms such as "holistic psychotherapy", "spiritual therapists" or "spiritual psychologists" to determine if someone in the state in which you live specializes in soul-related care. Many who show up in searches may be Christian-based counselors, but few will understand how to address matters of the soul. Instead, look for websites that use terminology similar to this book. Those practitioners are more likely to understand the services you need.

Keep in mind that most therapists and psychologists are licensed only in the state in which they live, so you may have to seek soul-based practitioners to gain additional assistance with the professionals you already see. In most cases, a whole soul care treatment team will still require the assistance of a medical practitioner to address the body-based aspects of anxiety (medication management, ketamine treatment, or other medically recognized modalities) and a psychological professional (therapist, counselor, clinical social worker, or psychologist who can help you address matters of the mind). Finally, one or more soul-healing practitioners may be integrated into your self-made treatment team to address various soul factors. While certain practitioners may specialize in one or more healing strategies, it is unusual to find a holistic practitioner who is skilled in all I mention in the root system of *The Whole Soul Model©*. You may not need but one practitioner to address the most essential factors, but like anything else, you won't know until you start your soul-based healing work.

In the future, I hope to see treatment teams include soul-healing specialists as part of all mental health care. This may become more formalized once certifications such as those I offer (*Soul Health Scholars* certifications) become more popular and recognized. My intention is to train practitioners of all fields to work together for the implementation of whole soul care.

Collaborating with Others

If you are a healthcare practitioner interested in integrating soul-based professionals into the care of clients, you may follow many of the suggestions listed above for patients. The days of one practitioner treating all aspects of a human are gone, but collaboration between you as a traditional practitioner and those who practice soul-based care is invaluable to providing effective and efficient assistance. While you don't have to fully understand every type of soul-based treatment, holding a willingness to interact and collaborate with holistic practitioners as part of a team will greatly benefit those you serve. Many basic webinars, books and videos exist to assist in learning more about certain soul-healing modalities. In the years to come, I intend to offer as many of these options as possible to inform practitioners about integrating all aspects of care for whole soul health.

Whole soul care requires professionals to build alliances with various holistic and soul-healing specialists who are able to contribute something you cannot. While you may be used to integrating with other professionals within the traditional system of care, it is understandable that you may be hesitant to do so with practitioners you know little about or exactly what they do. However, collaboration is one of the best ways to learn about developing techniques. It is certain that much more will evolve related to soul-healing in the years to come. You will be part of the blaze as new trails are forged to treating anxiety and other mental health concerns.

Monitoring Care

Like any other concern, care must be monitored in order to ensure that progress is maintained. Sometimes more layers of soul-based factors arise as healing already-identified wounds takes place. Similar to the peeling of an onion, our souls accumulate layers of wounds, fractures, and fragments along the way. Because healing one wound tends to make room for others to arise, the process might continue until the soul feels mostly healed.

I acknowledge that there are hazards to healing. I call these the hazards of evolution. First, the more you learn and grow, the more you want to learn and grow. There is something about shedding old wounds that excites and empowers us to continue the healing process. I tell clients that nothing surfaces unless it is supposed to: our soul knows when it is time to heal a wound that has remained dormant, sometimes for quite some time— including many lifetimes. While no one wants to experience the discomfort of healing, everyone I know wants to heal once they understand how this helps a person evolve. Although it is said that the human body has evolved about as much as it is going to, our soul has an infinite potential for growth. Each lifetime gives us the opportunity to evolve beyond the struggles we experience, making us both better humans and more conscious souls. Just as our soul helps us to survive even the harshest and most difficult conditions, it also wants to thrive as it heals and evolves.

Monitoring progress is part of any healing process. As noted in the soul factors of *The Whole Soul Model©*, Soul Mastery and Integration are our end goal—it is the final milestone of our experience within the human condition. What comes next is something even more grand—something to be discussed in future books.

Simply put, if any treatment, whether related to the body, mind or soul isn't working, it is important to stop, reassess and redirect your attention. Keep in mind, not all holistic practitioners understand the entirety of the whole soul experience, but some will provide pieces of the puzzle that could point you in the right direction.

Summing Up the Soul

It goes without saying that I believe the soul should be top priority when treating any condition, whether experienced by the body or mind. Both and more affect anxiety.

When fields of medicine and psychology began, the founding fathers of both emphasized the importance of the soul. Now, neither addresses it nor focuses care on the essence of who we really are. Our inner ally is the most unique and vital part of us, yet it has not only been minimized, it has been forgotten.

To complete this book, it feels important to share the concepts that first put the soul on the medical map. Socrates spoke of four arguments that he felt proved the everlastingness of the soul.

1. The first is called the *Cyclical Argument*, emphasizing the concept of opposites in explaining the presence of the soul. Socrates based this concept on the observation that all forms are everlasting and constant, which mirrors the idea that everything is energy. To him, the soul is responsible for bringing life, this also indicates that the soul is both immortal and imperishable. While the body *is* mortal and perishable, the soul is seen as something completely the opposite—it is both immortal and indestructible.

2. Socrates also posits an argument he called the *Theory of Recollection*. Because every living being holds certain non-empirical or practical knowledge at the

time of birth, this implies that the soul existed prior to this life since the information is carried forward.

3. His third argument is the *Argument from Affinity*, which is based on the fact that the soul is imperceptible, eternal and ethereal and varies from the body, which is perceptible, not eternal and corporeal or physical in nature. He emphasized that even though the body dies, our soul lives eternally.

4. The final argument emphasizes that all ethereal and constant entities are the origin of all things in the universe and everything in the world involves themselves in these forms. He argued that because the soul is imperishable and immortal in nature, it participates in the "Form" of life, which indicates that the soul is immortal.

Socrates was a philosopher, not a physician. History isn't clear whether he knew Hippocrates, who was considered the father of medicine. But both shared the opinion that the soul existed in everything related to the body. While Socrates was afflicted with temporal lobe epilepsy, there was no evidence that he had a mental illness. Hippocrates didn't seem to have any detectable physical illness. Although it is generally accepted that he lived to a healthy old age, no information is available to describe any physical or emotional conditions nor his death. Both Socrates and Hippocrates are known for their early contributions to the field of medicine, which planted the seeds for the evolution of medical tradition. While Hippocrates is still celebrated as the founding father of medicine, his original ideas about the core essence of life have somehow dissolved. I'm still baffled that medicine started with the soul, but dropped it along the way. I'm even more baffled that it has taken this long to bring it back.

While the field of medicine was birthed with the soul in mind, the idea of it somehow died as the field evolved. It is time for the essence of who we are to come back into the equation of health. It is time the soul finds a new birth.

The evolution of both research and theory about the body and mind treatment of anxiety has slowed. However, the treatment of the soul is soon to take off. Although early physicians and philosophers emphasized the importance of this vital force, they didn't know how to treat it. The evolution of the field now requires us to revisit its foundation, while incorporating the most important part—the roots of the soul in healing.

Body, mind *and* soul treatment of anxiety-related disorders is the only future. It is the only way to find whole soul health.

POST SCRIPT

Just when I think I've covered all of the bases regarding soul health, I realize there are more layers that could be discussed. While several books for this series are already in the works, writing *Anxiety: Treating Body, Mind and Soul* expanded my awareness about many other challenges we experience as part of the human condition and how to explain them using the various soul factors described in this book. For example, as I wrote about the impact of gender heritage as a possible initiator of unexplained anxiety, I saw more clearly how male souls have had to shut down their emotions and soul consciousness throughout the generations in order to survive. As a psychologist and therapist, this provided much insight into male vs. female roles in modern relationships and the struggles each has to understand one another.

While writing this book, I also embarked on completing the expansion of *The Soul Health Model*™. This resulted in a whole new image called *The Whole Soul Model*©. While I work with the soul every day, even I was astounded to recognize how many more factors influence us as part of the human condition than were ever taught in graduate school. We didn't even talk about the soul as part of medical education when I was a professor, which is a shame for so many reasons.

I also created images for both *The Soul-Informed Care Model*© and *The Three Levels of Healing*. I've spoken about these for years, but never thought to put a visual context around the concepts before. It was powerful for me to visualize the expansiveness of the soul and has been even more powerful for others with whom I've shared these images. Everyone has said that these models are just what practitioners, coaches and educators need right now to better understand why resolution of symptoms has been such a challenge.

Further, I realized that much of emotional health is influenced by the global evolution of man/womankind. For instance, the current astrological era called the Age of Aquarius has long been predicted to be both a time of tremendous transformation, especially spiritual expansion, and also one of turmoil and change. Several astrologers have told me in the last few years that the planets are aligned exactly as they were during the Revolutionary War. To those who understand planetary alignment and the impact it has on mood, global behavior and overall consciousness, this is something to keep an eye on. This energetic alignment inevitably impacts human emotion, coping and perspective along with how people treat one another. We are already seeing tremendous upheaval, discord and division which will inevitably cause more stress for everyone involved. That means 8.6 billion souls on this planet will be affected.

As I mentioned in this book, scientists believe the human body has evolved about as much as it will, give or take a few factors such as weight, life expectancy and ability to tolerate environmental influences including chemicals, electromagnetic frequencies emitted by electronics and other less known factors. It seems the more "advanced" society becomes, the more artificial it turns out to be as well—everything from food to intelligence displayed in technology. It is no wonder the soul gets left out given it is the most authentic part of who we are.

We have an uphill climb in understanding how humans tick, but hopefully *The Whole Soul Model©* will serve as a tool to expand our perspective.

For those who want to learn more about how mental health might be influenced by the various soul-related factors, the following pages provide descriptions of the next few books in *The Soul of Psychology* Series. Practitioners, coaches, educators and administrators who want to integrate soul health into the services they provide to others will also find more information about my *Soul Health Scholar Certifications*. You may also go to www.drkatherinetkelly.com/for-professional-development/.

Various video series are also available on my YouTube channel www.youtube.com/user/DrKTKelly. If you would like up-to-date information regarding events, guest appearances on podcasts, Soul Health Essentials—Oils of Evolution (www.soulhealthessentials.com) or books included in my Soul Health Series www.drkatherinetkelly.com/books you can sign up on www.drkatherinetkelly.com.

To know your soul is to know true health. Only then do you reach radiant living. Now is the time to honor your innermost ally to experience whole soul health.

REFERENCES

A Note from the Author

Abraham, M. 2020. A Brief History of Anxiety. Accessed September 2023.https://calmclinic/brief-history-of-anxiety.

Barsu, C. 2017. History of Medicine Between Tradition and Modernity. Clujul Medicine. 90(2):243-245.

Cherry, K. 2022. The Origins of Psychology: From Philosophical Beginnings to the Modern Day. Very Well Mind. Accessed September 2023. www.verywellmind.com/a-brief-history-of-psychology-through-the-years-2795245.

Post, S. & Puchalski, C.M. 2000. Physicians and Patient Spirituality: Professional Boundaries, Competency, and Ethics. Annals of Internal Medicine. 132:578.

Puchalski, C.M. 2001. The Role of Spirituality in Healthcare. Baylor University Medical Center Proceedings. 14: 352-357.

Chapter One

Abraham, M. 2020. A Brief History of Anxiety. Calm Clinic. Accessed September 2023. https://calmclinic.com/brief-history-of-anxiety.

Boland, M. 2023. The History of Anxiety. Psych Central. Accessed September 2023. https://psychcentral.com/anxiety/the-origins-of-anxiety#diagnosis.

Cherry, K. 2022. A Historical Timeline of Modern Psychology: A Brief Look at the People and Events that Shaped Modern Psychology. Very Well Mind. Accessed September 2023. https://verywellmind.com/timeline-of-modern-psychology-2795599.

Cherry, K. 2022. The Origins of Psychology: From Philosophical Beginnings to Modern Day. Very Well Mind. Accessed September 2023. https://verywellmind.com/a-brief-history-of-psycholog-through-the-years.

Crocq, M.A. 2015. A history of anxiety: From Hippocrates to DSM. Dialogues of Clinical Neuroscience, 17(3): 319-325.

Edelstein, L. 1943. The Hippocratic Oath: Text, Translation and Interpretation. John's Hopkins Press. Baltimore.

Hankinson, R. J. 1991. Galen's Anatomy of the Soul. Phronesis, 36(2): 197-233.

Jung, C.G., Dell, W.S. & Baynes, C.F. 1955. Modern Man in Search of a Soul. Harcourt Brace. New York.

Puchalski, C. 2001. The Role of Spirituality in Healthcare. Baylor University Medical Center Proceedings. 14: 352-357.

Puchalski, C & Ferrell, B.R. 2010. Making Healthcare Whole: Integrating Spirituality into Patient Care. Templeton Press, West Conshohocken PA.

Suris. A, Holliday R., & North, C.S. 2016. The Evolution of the Classification of Psychiatric Disorders. Journal of Behavioral Science. 6(1):5.

Chapter Two

Jung, C.G., Dell, W.S. & Baynes, C.F. 1955. Harcourt Brace. Modern Man in Search of a Soul. Harcourt Brace. New York.

Kelly, K.T. 2018. Soul Health: Aligning with Spirit for Radiant Living, Revised Second Edition. Soul Health Press. Winston-Salem, North Carolina.

Sanders, Irene T. I. 2003. What is Complexity? Complexsys.org. Accessed Sept 2023. https://complexsys.org/downloads/whatiscomplexity.pdf.

Chapter Three

American Psychiatric Association. 2013. DSM Changes from DSM-IV-TR to DSM-5. Accessed October 2023. www.psychiatry.org/File%20Library/Psychiatrists/Practice/DSM/APA_DSM_Changes_from_DSM-IV-TR_-to_DSM-5.pdf.

Crocq, MA. 2015. A History of Anxiety: From Hippocrates to DSM. Dialogues of Clinical Neuroscience, 17(3): 319-325.

Hankinson, R. J. 1991. Galen's Anatomy of the Soul. Phronesis, 36(2): 197-233.

Harriman, G.R. 2015. A Brief History of Anxiety & Fear. Explorable. Accessed October 2023. https://explorable.com/e/history-of-anxiety-and-fear.

Chapter Four

Abbott, R. & Lavretsky, H. 2013. Tai Chi and Qigong for the Treatment and Prevention of Mental Disorders. Psychiatry Clinics of North America. 36(1): 109–119.

Abraham, M. 2022. B Vitamins that Actually Work for Anxiety. Calm Clinic. Accessed October 2023. https://www.calmclinic.com/blog/calm-clinic-review-b-vitamins.

Blessing, E.M., Steenkamp, M.M., Manzanares, J. & Marmar, C. R. 2015. Cannabidiol as a Potential Treatment for Anxiety Disorders. Neurotherapeutics. 12: 825-836.

Blue, L. 2010. "Is Exercise the Best Drug for Depression?" Time Magazine Online. Accessed October 2023. https://content.time.com/time/health/article/0,8599,1998021,00.html.

Cirillo, P., et al. 2019. Transcranial Magnetic Stimulation in Anxiety and Trauma-Related Disorders: A systematic Review and Meta-Analysis. Brain Behavior. 9(6): e01284.

Cottone, J. & Moawad, H. 2023. Transcranial Magnetic Stimulation (TMS) for Anxiety: Is it Effective? Choosing Therapy. Accessed October 2023. www.choosingtherapy.com/tms-for-anxiety/.

Fiani, B. et. al. 2021. The Neurophysiology of Caffeine as a Central Nervous System Stimulant and the Resultant Effects on Cognitive Function. Cureus. 13(5): e15032.

Forbes, B. 2011. Yoga for Emotional Balance. Shambala: Boulder, CO.

Ghazizadeh, J., et al. 2021. The Effects of Lemon Balm (Melissa officinalis L.) on Depression and Anxiety in Clinical Trials: A Systematic Review and Meta-Analysis. Phytotherapy Research. 35(12):6690-6705.

Greiner-Ferris, J. & Khalsa, M. 2017. The Yoga-CBT Workbook for Anxiety. New Harbinger Publications: Oakland, California.

Hilimire, M.R., DeVylder, J.E., & Forestell, C.A. 2015. Fermented Foods, Neuroticism, and Social Anxiety: An interaction Model. Psychiatry Research. 228(2):203-8.

Katarzyna, J., Wojtkowska, K., Jakubszyk, K., Antoniewicz, J., & Skonieczna-Zydecka, K. 2020.Passiflora Incarnata in Neuropsychiatric Disorders: A Systematic Review. Nutrients.12(12): 3894.

Kiecolt-Glaser, J.K., Belury, M.A., Andridge, R., Malarkey, W.B. & Glase, R. 2011. Omega-3 Supplementation Lowers Inflammation and Anxiety in Medical Students: A Randomized Controlled Trial. Brain Behavior and Immunity. 25(8): 1725-34.

Klevebrant, L. & Frick, A. 2022. Effects of Caffeine on Anxiety and Panic Attacks in Patients with Panic Disorder: A Systematic Review and Meta-Analysis. General Hospital Psychiatry. 74:22-31.

Lake, J. 2018. How Exercise Reduces Anxiety. Psychology Today. Accessed October 2023. https://www.psychologytoday.com/us/blog/integrative-mental-health-care/201810/how-exercise-reduces-anxiety.

Li, A.W. & Goldsmith, C. W. 2012. The Effects of Yoga on Anxiety and Stress. Alternative Medicine Review. 17(1):21-35.

Massimo, E. M. 2021. 5-Hyroxytroptophan (5-HTP): Natural Occurrence, Analysis, Biosynthesis, Biotechnology, Physiology and Toxicology. International Journal of Molecular Science. 22(1): 181.

Mayo Clinic. 2017. Depression and Anxiety: Exercise Eases Symptoms. Accessed October 2023. https://www.mayoclinic.org/diseases-conditions/depression/in-depth/depression-and-exercise/art-20046495.

Mayo Clinic. 2023. Anxiety Disorders: Symptoms and Causes. Accessed October 2023.www.mayoclinic.org/diseases-conditions/anxiety/symptoms-causes/syc-20350961.

Office of Disease Prevention and Health Promotion. 2023. Physical Activity Guidelines for Americans. Accessed October 2023. https://health.gov/our-work/nutrition-physial-activity/physical-activity-guidelines.

Paluska, S.A. & Schwenk, T.L. 2000. Physical Activity and Mental Health: Current Concepts. Sports Medicine. 29(3): 167-80.

Reiff, C.M., et. al. 2020. Psychedelics and Psychedelic-Assisted Psychotherapy. American Journal of Psychiatry. 177:391–410.

Russo, A.J. 2011. Decreased Zinc and Increased Copper in Individuals with Anxiety. Sage Journals Accessed October 2023. https://journals.sagepub.com/doi/10.4137/NMI.S6349.

Sanders, Irene T.I. 2003. What is Complexity? Accessed Sept 2023. https://complexsys.org/downloads/whatiscomplexity.pdf.

Sherman, K.J., et al. 2010. Effectiveness of Therapeutic Massage for Generalized Anxiety Disorder: A Randomized Controlled Trial. Depression and Anxiety. 27(5): 441–450.

Schinsuke, H. et al. 2019. Effects of L-Theanine Administration on Stress-Related Symptoms andCognitive Functions in Healthy Adults: A Randomized Controlled Trial. Nutrients. 11(10):2362.

Strohle, A. 2009. Physical Activity, Exercise, Depression and Anxiety Disorders. Journal of Neural Transmission. 116(6) (2009): 777-84.

Weil, A. (2011). Spontaneous Happiness. Little, Brown and Company. New York.

Yang, X.Y., Yang, N.B., Huang, F.F., et al. 2021. Effectiveness of Acupuncture on Anxiety Disorder: A Systematic Review and Meta-Analysis of Randomized Controlled Trials. Annals of General Psychiatry. 20: 9.

Chapter Five

Benson, H. & Klipper, M.Z. 2000. The Relaxation Response, Expanded Updated Edition. Harper Collins Publishers. New York.

Curtin, R.R. 2015. Psychotherapeutic Reiki: A Holistic Body-Mind Approach to Psychotherapy. Keystroke Studios. Cambridge, Massachusetts.

Hayes, S.C., Strosahl, K.D., & Wilson, K.G. 2016. Acceptance and Commitment Therapy: The Process and Practice of Mindful Change. Guilford Press. New York.

Hofmann, S.G. & Gomez, A.F. 2017. Mindfulness-Based Interventions for Anxiety and Depression. Psychiatry Clinics of North America. 40(4): 739–749.

Kabat-Zinn, J., 2013. Full Catastrophe Living: Using the Wisdom of your Body and Mind to Ease Pain, Stress and Illness. Random House. New York.

Lake, J. 2018. How Exercise Reduces Anxiety. Psychology Today. Accessed October 2023. https://www.psychologytoday.com/us/blog/integrative-mental-health-care/201810/how-exercise-reduces-anxiety.

Luoma, J. 2019. Key Differences Between Acceptance and Commitment Therapy (ACT) and Radically Open Dialectical Behavioral Therapy (RO DBT). Accessed December 2023.www.actwithcompassion.com/key_differences_between_act_and_ro_dbt.

Markowitz, J.C. & Wiessman, M.M. 2012. Interpersonal Psychotherapy: Past, Present and Future. Clinical Psychology and Psychotherapy. 9(2): 99–105.

McKay, M., Wood, J.C. & Brantley, J. 2019. The Dialectical Behavior Therapy Skills Workbook: Practical DBT Exercises for Learning Mindfulness, Interpersonal Effectiveness, Emotional Regulation. Harbinger Publications. California.

Pitman, S. R. & Knauss, D.P.C. 2020. Contemporary Psychodynamic Approaches to Treating Anxiety: Theory, Research and Practice. Advanced Experiments in Medical Biology. 1191:451-464.

Scelles, C. & Bulnes, L.C. 2021. EMDR as Treatment Option for Conditions Other Than PTSD: A Systematic Review. Frontiers in Psychology. 12: 644369.

Schimelpfening, N. 2023. Dialectical Behavior Therapy (DBT): Definition, Techniques, and Benefits. Accessed October 2023. https://www.verywellmind.com/dialectical-behavior-therapy-1067402.

Chapter Six

May, Rollo. 1994. The Discovery of Being: Writings in Existential Psychology. (Reprint) W.W. Norton & Company. New York.

Chapter Seven

Singh, M. 2017. The Cultural Evolution of Shamanism. Pub Med. Accessed November 2023. https://www.pubmed.ncbi.nlm.nih.gov/28679454/.

Chapter Eight

Kelly: K.T. 2018. Soul Health: Aligning with Spirit for Radiant Living, Revised Second Edition. Soul Health Press. Winston-Salem, North Carolina.

Chapter Nine

Center for Disease Control and Prevention. What is Epigenetics? Center for Disease Control. Accessed Jan 2024. www.cdc.gov/genomics/disease/epigenetics.htm.

Darwin, C. 1958. The Autobiography of Charles Darwin: 1809-1882. W.W. Norton & Company, Ltd. New York.

Friedman. H.L. & Hartelius, G. 2015. The Wiley-Blackwell Handbook of Transpersonal Psychology. John Wiley & Sons. New York.

Rubik, B., Muehsam, D., Hammerschlag, R. & Jain, S. 2015. Biofield Science and Healing: History, Terminology and Concepts. Global Advancements in Health Medicine. 4:8-14.

Chapter Ten

Foor, D. 2017. Ancestral Medicine: Rituals for Personal and Family Healing. Bear & Company. Rochester, Vermont.

Ingerman, S. 2015. Walking in Light: The Everyday Empowerment of a Shamanic Life. Sounds True. Boulder, Colorado.

MacLeod, A. 2019. The Old Soul's Guidebook: Who You Are, Why You're Here, & How toNavigate Life on Earth. Soul World Press. Vashon, Washington.

Moreno, J. 2019. Psychodrama. Psychodrama Press. Princeton, New Jersey.

Myss, C. 2003. Sacred Contracts: Awakening Your Divine Potential. Harmony Books. New York.

Schwartz, R. 2023. An Introduction to Internal Family Systems. Sounds True. Boulder, Colorado.

Tolle, E., 2004. The Power of Now: A Guide to Spiritual Enlightenment. New World Library. Novato, California.

Woolfolk, J.M. 2012. The Only Astrology Book You'll Ever Need. Taylor Trade Publishing. Lanham, Maryland.

Chapter Eleven

American Psychiatric Association. 2022. Diagnostic and Statistical Manual of Mental Disorders, Text Revision, DSM-5-TR, Fifth Edition. Washington, D. C.

Bandoim, L. 2023. How Anxiety Disorder is Diagnosed. Very Well Health. www.verywellhealth.com/anxiety-disorder-diagnosis-5114303.

Beck, A.T., Epstein, N. Brown, G. & Steer, R. A. 1988. An Inventory for Measuring Clinical Anxiety: Psychometric Properties. Journal of Consulting Clinical Psychology. 56(6): 893-7.

Mughal, A.Y., Devadas, J., Ardman, E., Levis, B., Go, V.F. & Gaynes, B.N. 2020. A Systematic Review of Validated Screening Tools for Anxiety Disorders and PTSD in Low to Middle Income Countries. BMC Psychiatry. 20: 338.

Spielberger, C. D., Gorsuch, R. L., Lushene, R., Vagg, P. R., & Jacobs, G. A. 1983. Manual for the State-Trait Anxiety Inventory. Consulting Psychologists Press. Palo Alto, California.

Spitzer, R.L., Kroenke, K., Williams, J.B.W. & Lowe, B. 2006. A Brief Measure for Assessing Generalized Anxiety Disorder. Archives of Internal Medicine. 166:1092-1097.

Chapter Twelve

Burger, J. 2023. Americans are Surprisingly Spiritual, New Study Finds. Aleteia. Accessed January 2023. www.aleteia.org/2023/12/14/americans-are-surprisingly-spiritual-new-study-finds/.

Conner, J. 2021. Writing Down Your Soul: How to Activate and Listen to the Extraordinary Voice Within. Mango Publishing Group. Coral Gables, Florida.

Curtin, R.R. 2015. Psychotherapeutic Reiki: A Holistic Body-Mind Approach to Psychotherapy. Keystroke Studios. Cambridge, Massachusetts.

Dale, C. 2014. The Subtle Body: An Encyclopedia of Our Energetic Anatomy. Sounds True. Boulder, Colorado.

Foor, D. 2017. Ancestral Medicine: Rituals for Personal and Family Healing. Bear & Company. Rochester, Vermont.

Friedman. H.L. & Hartelius, G. 2015. The Wiley-Blackwell Handbook of Transpersonal Psychology. John Wiley & Sons. New York.

Gunaratana, B.H. 2011. Mindfulness in Plain English, 20th Anniversary Edition. Wisdom Publications. Somerville, Massachusetts.

Hamaker-Zondag, K. 1990. Psychological Astrology: A Synthesis of Jungian Psychology and Astrology. Weiser Books. Newburyport, Massachusetts.

Harris, M., Fallot, R.D. 2001. Envisioning a Trauma-Informed Service System: A Vital Paradigm Shift. New Directions for Mental Health Services. (89): 3-22.

Ingerman, S. 2006. Soul Retrieval: Mending the Fragmented Self, Revised, Updated Edition. Harper One. New York.

Ingerman, S. 2015. Walking in Light: The Everyday Empowerment of a Shamanic Life. Sounds True. Boulder, Colorado.

Jung, C.G., Dell, W.S. & Baynes, C.F. 1955. Modern Man in Search of a Soul. Harcourt Brace. New York.

Laszlo, E. 2007. Science and the Akashic Field: An Integral Theory of Everything, Second Edition. Inner Traditions. Rochester, Vermont.

Maslow, A. 2013. Theory of Human Motivation, Reprint. Martino Publishing. Mansfield Centre, Connecticut.

Miller, R.L. 2017. Psychedelic Medicine: The Healing Powers of LSD, MDMA, Psilocybin, and Ayahuasca. Park Street Press Rochester, Vermont.

Mischke-Reeds, M. 2018. Somatic Psychotherapy Toolbox: 125 Worksheets and Exercised to Treat Trauma & Stress. Professional Education Systems Institute. Eau Clare, Wisconsin.

Pew Research Center. 2023. Spirituality Among Americans. Pew Research Center. Accessed January 2024. www.pewresearch.org/religion/2023/12/07/spirituality-among-americans/.

Van der Kolk, B. 2015. The Body Keeps the Score: Brain, Mind, and Body in the Healing of Trauma. Penguin Books. London.

Weiss, B. 1988. Many Lives, Many Masters: The True Story of a Prominent Psychiatrist, His Young Patient, and the Past-Life Therapy That Changed Both Their Lives. Simon & Schuster, Inc. New York.

Weiss, B. 2005. Same Soul, Many Bodies: Discover the Healing Power of Future Lives Through Progression Therapy. Free Press. New York.

Chapter Fourteen

Sena, W. 2022. Socrates' Four Arguments for the Immortality of the Soul in the Phaedo: Informal Fallacies, Ambiguities, and Overall Inconsistency. Harvard Library. Accessed January 2024. https://dash.harvard.edu/handle/1/373889.

ABOUT THE AUTHOR

DR. KATHERINE T. KELLY, Ph.D., M.S.P.H. is a clinical and holistic health psychologist, former Director of Behavioral Science in Family/Community Medicine and medical school professor, best-selling author, speaker, consultant, and soul-healing specialist with over thirty-eight years of service in mental health and wellness.

Dr. Kelly was named "the pioneer of soul health" following the publication of her first book, *Soul Health: Aligning with Spirit for Radiant Living*, which showcased her trademarked Soul Health Model. Her book gained best-selling status following the release of her second edition. She went on to author *The Recipe for Radiance: Mastering the Art and Soul of Self-Care*, which provides a much-needed guide to creating a personalized and life-long "soul care" plan. Her most recent book, *The Healer's Path to Post-COVID Recovery: A Restorative Journey for Healthcare Workers*, reached best-selling status in eight Amazon categories for newly published books and earned two awards (Living Now Books Bronze Award Winner and Nautilus Books Silver Award Winner with a special "Rise to the Moment" category).

Her new book, *Anxiety: Treating Body, Mind and Soul*, is the first in her Soul of Psychology series, which emphasizes the need to expand both the conceptualization and treatment of mental health disorders to include what she calls "Soul-Informed Care". This series stresses the importance of including all aspects of a person's health—the body, mind and soul—to understand the root causes of particular mental health conditions. No other author has so clearly identified the soul factors responsible for tough-to-treat concerns.

Dr. Kelly lives in Winston-Salem, NC and has taught her Soul Health Model™ throughout the United States. To learn more or to contact Dr. Kelly, visit www.drkatherinetkelly.com.

THE SOUL OF PSYCHOLOGY SERIES

The Soul of Psychology Series elevates the core origin of a person's experience of common mental health-related conditions to the forefront, bringing the essence of an individual back to the center of treatment rather than the symptoms that have come to define them. This completes the picture of healing action through not only body and mind, but most importantly, soul as well.

For years, we've relied on the fields of modern medicine and psychology to answer the toughest questions of why we struggle in life and how to manage various emotional concerns. Now it is time to re-establish the health of the soul as the primary element in true healing.

This series examines all aspects of a person's health—body, mind, AND soul—to assist in returning an individual to whole health. Without attention to all root causes of a condition, treatment will continue only as a management of symptoms rather than a permanent resolution of that which leaves a person feeling less than complete.

The Soul of Psychology Series creates the foundation for a much-needed whole and soul health approach to many of the most common medical and psychological concerns.

The next book in this series
Depression: Treating Body, Mind and Soul
Book Two

Depression is the world's second leading mental health concern, but for many it could easily be renamed "suppression of the soul." ***Depression: Treating Body, Mind and Soul*** explains the deeper origins of this often-elusive concern. The essence of who we are—the soul—can become so wounded that our external experience of life can be greatly dampened.

Dr. Katherine T. Kelly, Ph.D., M.S.P.H. elevates the understanding of mental health concerns through bridging up-to-date scientific research related to the body and mind aspects of healing depression with the less-known soul-based factors that often affect some patients. Topics such as epigenetic factors and ancestral trauma related to mood, past-life events like the experience of famine, war, or epidemics such as a plague or other tragic health crisis, unexplained difficulties with family or partner relationships, and other soul-based factors are discussed.

This book enhances the conceptualization of depressive conditions to include the body, mind, and soul as essential elements in healing. ALL factors must be explored and addressed for complete healing to occur.

Upcoming books in the Soul of Psychology Series

PTSD: Treating Body, Mind and Soul

Grief: Treating Body, Mind and Soul

Obsessive-Compulsive Disorders: Treating Body, Mind and Soul

Feeding and Eating Disorders: Treating Body, Mind and Soul

Sleep-Wake Disorders: Treating Body, Mind and Soul

Personality Disorders: Treating Body, Mind and Soul

Relationships: Treating Body, Mind and Soul

Other Books by Dr. Katherine T. Kelly
The Soul Health Series

Soul Health: Aligning with Spirit for Radiant Living describes how the soul is at the hub of all aspects of our health and well-being and provides the roadmap to reaching optimal health—soul health. Using her trademarked Soul Health Model, Dr. Kelly provides the framework for achieving ultimate balance and fulfillment in your everyday life and provides self-empowerment tools to assist in your soul's evolution. ***Soul Health*** serves as both an instructional guide and workbook as readers create their path to radiant health.

Recipe for Radiance: Mastering the Art and Soul of Self-Care reveals the secret ingredients to living your most radiant life. As an expert in Soul Health, Dr. Katherine T. Kelly knows that self-care is soul care. She offers a master soul-care plan you can use to restore your body, recharge your mind, inspire your soul, and transform your life. The metaphor of creating your own perfect recipe takes shape throughout this book, leaving you with a life-enriching, personalized plan for nurturing yourself.

In ***The Healer's Path to Post-COVID Recovery: A Restorative Journey for Healthcare Workers,*** Dr. Kelly uses her nationally-known Soul Health Model to provide tools for healing from this life-altering pandemic. She also shares powerful stories of strength, suffering, courage, and compassion from the nearly 150 traditional and holistic healthcare providers she interviewed. Dr. Kelly wrote this book to help readers realign and rebalance their lives following the dark night of healthcare's soul. ***The Healer's Path*** is a Living Now Books Bronze Award Winner and Nautilus Books Silver Award Winner in a special "Rise to the Moment" category.

Coming in 2025
Soul Health Scholars Certifications

Soul Health Scholar Certifications are designed to assist practitioners, coaches, educators, and administrators to understand and integrate Soul-Informed Care into the services they provide to others. Scholars become proficient in using Dr. Kelly's trade-marked Soul Health Model™, Whole Soul Model©, Soul-Informed Care Model© and various soul-based healing methods that are reflected in these models.

Participants benefit from understanding the dynamic interplay between the various "branches" of health and how a client or patient's progress can be inhibited or blocked when these facets of health and well-being are misaligned. In-depth discussion about each branch of the human condition is included and suggestions are offered for ways to work with clients and patients to eliminate obstacles to creating their optimal life.

Both holistic and spiritual elements of healing (introduction to energy healing, influence of "soul wounds" on client progress, etc.) are discussed to prepare for deeper integration of the services you already offer. As part of this training, Dr. Kelly works with participants to experience their own realignment process as she conducts a comprehensive "Soul Health Assessment", which teaches scholars how to implement a Soul Health Plan with clients and patients. Various soul-healing strategies and techniques are discussed.

While licensed practitioners, coaches, educators and administers receive a renewable certification, others are also invited to participate to enhance their own overall health. For more information, visit www.drkatherinetkelly.com/for-professional-development/.

Made in the USA
Middletown, DE
24 August 2024